I0568395

How to
Have
Fun
with
Your
Fear

How to Have Fun with Your Fear

SHARE YOUR BRAVE WORDS AND CHANGE THE WORLD

LAURA DI FRANCO

©2021 by Laura Di Franco

All rights reserved.
This book may not be reproduced in whole or in part without the written permission front he publisher, except by a reviewer who may quote brief passages in a review; nor may any part of this book be reproduced, stored in a retrieval system, or transmitted in any form or by any means, electronic, mechanical, photocopying, recording or other, without written permission from the publisher.

Paperback: ISBN: 978-1-954047-02-0
eBook: ISBN: 978-1-954047-09-9

Printed in the United States of America

Dedication

To my daughter, without whom I wouldn't truly understand the definition of brave. I love you so much. And to the divine posse who helped me step back into my worth and power, feel the fear, do it anyway, and have way more fun with what scares me so I could get on with my mission of changing the world, I'm so honored to be in your badass company. Thank you.

Table of Contents

Introduction

Having fun with your fear is about cultivating a badass kind of awareness. This book will help with that.

Your fear is boring.

ELIZABETH GILBERT

When I read Elizabeth Gilbert's Facebook post titled, "Your Fear is Boring," I was hit so hard in the solar plexus with a feeling of inspired energy, I sat up a little straighter. My awareness was on point. I noticed that this meant something to me. Something huge.

I then proceeded to have the initials Y F I B tattooed on my forearm in the middle of a feather as a life-long reminder to give up on the boring fears that have paralyzed me for so long and kept me from living the juicy, wild, sexy, passionate, adventurous life I've always known was waiting just on the other side of that fear.

It was that big of a deal for me.

I've changed the quote to make it my own: *Your fear of not-good-enough is boring.*

A special thank you to LG for writing that bit of awesomeness that day and lighting a fire in me that's fueled a revolution of Brave Healing.

Brave Healing

How about we do some Brave Healing right now.

I'm going to show you how.

Rest your mind,
take a breath,
feel the words that are said.

Drop down inside,
recognize: hiding isn't the answer.

Take a moment to feel everything.
Maybe you'll see we all feel everything.

Nothing's really right or wrong,
it's all more like a song.
You like rock,
I like jazz,
But all music has a vibe
and it's the vibe we feel that's real.

No word or rhyme or melody is better
it all just depends on what jives with your heart
what makes your soul light on fire,
or dance
or sing
or express.

So maybe instead of killing each other
or dropping bombs
or trying to find something the other did wrong,
we could move to the sounds made of love.

How about we heal the wound inside ourselves first?
That's the way we heal the world.

What if being born automatically makes you worthy,
a living, breathing manifestation of creative energy
with the power to heal.
It all starts with a feel.

You're a healer whether you know it or not;
might as well be brave and start now.
What do you feel?

Can you feel yourself out loud on the stage with your message?
Or does the heat of unworthiness and shame keep you afraid?

Fear is just a feeling
and it's stealing your show.
It's going to take a brave kind of healing.
But I am here today to tell you
that anything is possible
when you wake up,
fiercely alive,
inside of your life,
and decide to make a change.

Brave Healing.
It starts with a pause,
and a breath.
A check-in with your bod
and your mind,
knowing what feels good and right to your soul.

Follow those sacred breadcrumbs
until you're standing there
staring joy in the face
and both of you laugh and say,
"Baby, we've mastered this game,
Now it's time to play!"

For more Brave Healer poetry visit https://www.Facebook.com/WarriorLove

Dear Brave Reader,

As a healer you've chosen a warrior's path: to battle your fears, heal your wounds, and trail-blaze the way for others. Congratulations on being one of a small group of individuals who are changing the world in this way.

Interestingly enough, warriors are not fearless. We sometimes do life with the deepest wounds and the most fear. Thing is, we were born for this journey, and we've woken up to our calling, mission, and purpose.

It's time we stand up inside our worthiness, embody our expertise, and begin to serve the world in a new, bigger way.

If you're ready to take your healing game to the next level, have way more fun with your fear, and start stepping up to share your message out loud with those you're meant to serve, then you're in the right place. Grab my hand.

Be ready to feel inspired. Be ready to feel the fire lit beneath you and your purpose in a way you've hoped for but couldn't create on your own. Be ready to receive the energy and nourishment that comes from serving from an overflow instead of your reserves—the only real way to help others.

This book is an Italian minestrone, made of all my fiery passion and all the tools I've learned about using fear as fuel. It's part law of attraction and part *The Motivation Manifesto*. It's *The Secret* and *A New Earth*. It's some martial art tenants, and it's habits of highly effective people. It's a lifetime's worth of awareness and self-development study and the tools to apply that knowledge to the fears you're so tired of. It's knowing how to shift fear energy into fuel for your wildest dreams.

I made my way to redefining healing, and reframing fear by waking up inside my own life, giving myself permission to feel the low-level resentment infecting my soul, and then making a decision to change it all.

I used the awareness and tools I learned as a healer, the discipline I practiced as a martial artist, and the intuition I re-learned as a mother, wife, employee, daughter, sister, lover, and passion-filled writer to get to the healing, clarity, and joy I knew was waiting for me.

If you're like me, you know there's more to life than what you're experiencing. You believe in the magic of soul, purpose, calling, vision, mission, and being. You feel an energy working in the background constantly that nudges you to go for it, to live out your dreams, to be the change.

If you're like me, you wake inspired, wanting to make a difference and believing in your ability to do so. And some days are better than others. Anxiety is constant. But you're starting to shift that.

If you are where I was a few short years ago, you're searching for that something more. You're exhausted by not being fully supported. You might be burning out or even feeling ill.

You're smelling smoke and hoping your house doesn't burn down. You might be afraid to speak up, afraid to ask for what you need, or afraid to make the change you know you need to make to live the life you're meant to live.

If you're in that place of noticing the messages your body is giving you and ignoring them, then you're living with the fear of what might happen to you if you continue like that.

There were many times I wondered if I'd have a heart attack and leave my children way too early because I was too afraid to do what I knew would make a better life for me and for them. I was afraid of the consequences of my actions hurting others or ruining someone else's life, while my own felt smaller, tighter, and more constricting.

You also might be living in constant fear of failure, trapped in a box you created, realizing you barely recognize yourself anymore.

Are you in the process of building your business and feeling the effects of trading your hours for dollars, knowing you won't last much longer but not knowing what to do about it?

Are you living by everyone else's rules about how to do your business or life because it's what you're supposed to do? Then you're most likely living with the fear of never truly living out your desires, dreams, and goals, on your own terms, in this lifetime. Life is short. The feeling of inspired urgency lives and breathes in the middle of your chest and gut and it has a voice:

There *is* more.

You *are* worthy of it all.

You *can* change everything.

Your message matters.

You *can* live the life you dream about.

And . . . you're about to learn how to get there.

It's time to have more fun with that fear, Brave Healer. Fear is just a feeling. You can feel it and take the action anyway. I'm going to help show you exactly how to do that.

Having fun with fear requires three steps: knowing what you want, feeling everything, and getting off your ass to take aligned action toward what you want, despite the voices in your head.

I know I make it sound super simple. And it *is*, if you think it is. Honestly, what if this could be easy? Start by asking yourself powerful questions that shake up what you think you already know.

A few years ago, it felt really hard for me. I was pissed, resentful, blaming my family and other people for my unhappiness. I had a big mission to help people heal, but within the confines of my mind, I created a prison with no door. I needed to heal me first.

Along with all the healing tools I've learned over my career, I've used journaling since I was fifteen and began to create my own healing tool: a combination of awareness, writing, and speaking out loud.

I had books inside me and in 2012 ended up self-publishing my first, *Living, Healing and Tae Kwon Do*, detailing a six-year journey of my life with my son as we trained together and finally earned our black belts.

Writing—and, more so, publishing—that book would end up kicking a pebble I didn't know I was kicking. I thought writing the book would be difficult, in terms of fear. Once I realized that people would actually read it, and I'd have to deal with all the feedback as well as my own inner critic messages, oh boy, the fear fun had just begun. Only it wasn't fun at all. It was paralyzing. And triggering. And it mostly made me sick to my stomach. Even worse, it kept me from taking the action I knew I needed to take to live the life I dreamt of.

But I kept writing. And feeling. And writing. And teaching. And writing. They say we teach what we most need to learn. I feel that.

In 2015, I had another book moving through me. I wrote out the story of my childhood wounds during NaNoWriMo, a free online writing program with the goal of finishing a 30,000-word book in thirty days.

I feng shui'd my soul on those pages, put the story down in black and white, and then attached what ended up being a a 65,000-word book that I titled *Love in a Nightmare* to an email addressed to my family and hit send on Christmas Eve.

You might be wondering, *Wait, what?* You might imagine what happened inside of me at that point. It felt like a combination of panic and relief.

The fear of my family's reaction—particularly their feelings of upset, disappointment, and offense—couldn't stop me from taking care of healing myself that day. My compass pointed toward taking action on something I knew needed to happen. Something that would catapult me into a career of helping others with their purpose-driven fear. And, believe it or not, that action spurred healing conversations between my family members. They didn't disown me. I still speak to all of them to this day!

That book ended up being the healing I needed to clear a space inside for the Brave Healing revolution that would ensue. It was the work I had to do for the next, real book I wrote, called *Brave Healing, a Guide for Your Journey*. Released in 2018, that book has been the leap I needed to take . . . a cannonball into fear, to make my much-bigger dreams a reality.

I've done many scary things since, including reciting my first poem from a microphone in the front of the room, drag racing my new car, starting a new business, and asking for a divorce. During the writing of this book, I would experience a #metoo situation way too close to home—making it necessary to begin to understand the world of the justice system and how to support someone I love through that—as well as my first pandemic. When your fears are put into perspective by bigger ones, everything changes. That recent shift in perspective inspired me to finish this book and get it out into the world to help others with the tools I've learned.

How was I able to take action through the heart-pounding, stomach-sickening, leg-weakening fear each time? I learned to feel the physical feeling, not make it mean anything, and get on with taking aligned action on something my soul told me to do, with an end goal of pure joy.

I practiced those steps until I created a new reaction inside of me that helps me, rather than paralyzes me. I trained myself to have fun with my fear. You can too.

Imagine a feeling of purpose inside, so big and bright and badass, it grabs fear by the hand and pulls it, skipping along with a smile on its face through the wall of fire to the other side without so much as a single singed hair? That's how we can be with our fear.

Fear is easy to be paralyzed by when you've settled for a mediocre life and nothing you want is worth the effort of feeling afraid and doing it anyway.

What you crave must burn brightly enough to hurt inside you. That pain is how you know you're alive. You have to want something and you have to want it bad enough to battle your fears.

And here's the thing; what you want may have changed over the years. Your original wants and desires may have been created by what you were taught you should want, or the rules, should's and supposed to's you learned would be the path to happiness.

You might be in the middle of waking up to the fact that what you thought you wanted does not feel like you thought it would. And you're starting to question it all. That's good!

It takes a warrior to wake up inside of her life and decide she needs to make a change.

This journey isn't for the faint of heart. I aim to grab the hands of you brave healers and help you know you're not doing this alone. It takes a special kind of person to choose this path and then keep choosing it, even when it feels impossible or it shoves you out of your comfort zone so far you've started to forget who and where you are.

Thankfully, you don't have to do this alone; I've gathered up an amazing group of Brave Healers in my free Facebook group. Join the revolution for more support as you read this book here: https://www.facebook.com/groups/1375571059231845/.

Controlling your thoughts is the first hurdle you have to overcome on this journey. What you think your life is like is how your life will be, until you think something better, healthier, and more aligned with your desires, dreams, and goals. For example, if you constantly think about being broke and alone, you're going to stay broke and alone. Habitual patterns of doubt, fear, uncertainty, shame, blame, sadness, etc., are what keep you paralyzed and not making any progress.

Fear will keep you paralyzed until you realize it's just a feeling and then do something better about it. It's time to do the healing work and build the discipline of awareness you'll need as the foundation for the kind of courage required to play bigger in the world.

There's science behind the fear that holds people back, but I've decided not to cover fear science in this book. It's been done. There's plenty of proof and scientific explanation out there for you to read about the why and how of all kinds of fear. I have left you a hearty list of books you can explore for this purpose in the resource guide at the end of the book.

Instead, this book intends to address what I call the purpose-driven kind of fear.

Your fear, feelings of "not good enough," and reluctance to go after what your soul is calling you to do are boring. It's time to make a change. It's time to take your gifts and put them into action so every moment of your life is lived fiercely alive, aware, and joyful, no matter what is happening around you.

Reading more about the science of fear might just be a distraction for the action you really need to take to make this happen. In fact, the pursuit of more knowledge and the quest for perfection is something that continues to get in the way of actually doing the practical work of being better. It gets in the way of the practice itself.

This book is about using purpose-driven fear as a compass, something to move toward, not away from. It's about overcoming the paralyzing and visceral grip your fear thoughts have over you and creating fuel from that energy. And it's about using that fuel to make your dreams of changing the world come true.

This book is for the healers ready to change themselves and in doing so know they're changing the world. It's for you if you're ready to take responsibility for everything in your life, create the change you want, and then share those gifts out loud so you're leaving the legacy you were born for.

Everyone is a healer. Might as well be brave and start now. And let's put our focus and attention on what matters: shifting the energy of fear to something that we can use as fuel. You're either moving through the world with a high-flying vibe or not. And with the proper awareness, it's always your choice.

Thank you for being here, for being brave, and for your willingness to do this adventure with me. Isn't it about time we get to have a little fun with our fear?

A quick note about how to get the most out of the book:

Make sure you have a pen and notebook handy; you'll be writing.

Having a group of friends who are doing the exercises with you is an excellent idea! When you create communities, you stay accountable to the work.

And make sure to join my free group on Facebook—Brave Badass Healers, a Community for World-Changers—so you can get some extra support and inspiration along the way.

Find some great next steps at www.BraveHealer.com as well!

Would you like me to come speak about the chapters at your book club? You know where to contact me!

Here's to having more fun with your fear!

With warrior love,

Laura

You Have to Know What You Want

Knowing what you want is key to having fun with fear, but it can be tricky. What you want now might be different than what you wanted in your twenties or thirties. Can you recognize the changes you've made? Do you know why you want what you want now? Or do things seem foggy, confused, or unclear?

The first four chapters will explore desire, purpose-driven fear, enthusiasm, and your thoughts—everything you need to place your intention on creating the playground you'll invite fear to have a playdate on. The awareness you'll cultivate in Part One is the foundation for the courage. Let's get to building that strong foundation!

Wild Desire

I notice where the summer breeze
touches my skin
and I begin
to come alive

where sun beams
warm my face
no trace
of want or worry

tweets and twitters
flutter through my mind
the world becomes kind
in sacred spaces

breath is hot
bothered
passion rises
surprising my tired soul

high from staring
at cloud-covered skies
drifting pictures
making love to my eyes

noticing how a moment
holds everything I need

to feel a deep
desperate fire

wild desire
reaches out
dancing bare
teasing intolerable dare

"play with me"
she whispers
behind my ear
sending shivers everywhere.

CHAPTER 1
Purpose-Driven Fear

So, what is purpose-driven fear? It's the kind of fear you know is getting in the way of your big, fat dreams.

Mine was preventing me from asking for a divorce, the thing I knew needed to happen if I was going to make any dream of mine come true in the future. I've been in the middle of fear, paralyzed, not knowing what the next best step is and terrified about what would happen if I didn't make a change. That's purpose-driven fear, and it often affects those of us who are in healing professions.

Reason being that the journey of a healer is unique. I look back on my decision to become a physical therapist at sixteen years of age and smile. The Universe had a plan for me all along. I think that's so cool. There are so many events in the past that help us move into being and doing what we're meant for.

In fact, start right now. Look back at the events you only now realize were perfectly orchestrated for you. Smile with me. There's a plan for you too. As you look back at all the events of your life, can you see the purpose in each of them, whether you judged them as good or bad in those moments? This kind of awareness makes life a lot more fun. And awareness is the foundation for the kind of courage you need to live the life you crave.

"Try to love the questions themselves as if they were locked rooms or books written in a very foreign language. Don't search for the answers, which could not be given to you now, because you would not be able to live with them. And the point is to live everything. Live the questions now."

—RAINER MARIA RILKE

I have a few questions for you . . .

Are you so busy healing and pleasing others you've forgotten about yourself?

Is the job you once raved about to your friends and family burning you out?

Are you afraid to say that out loud?

Are you feeling isolated, anxious, or lonely?

Are many of your moments spent dwelling in negative thoughts, resentments, worries, anxiety, or fear?

Are you afraid to speak up for what you really want?

Does fear paralyze you from doing what you want on a regular basis even though you know nothing truly bad is going to happen?

Sometimes it's hard to believe the Universe has a plan for us. In the intensity of our moments, we don't see the bigger picture. And we're afraid of so many things along the way. Maybe even that we've chosen the wrong career. Or husband. Or life.

When I started to veer from my usual love-what-I-do energy to one sounding more like *OMG, I'm not sure anymore, I'm tired,* I had to wake up a little and wonder. I had to ask myself some hard questions. I had to re-identify myself. And it felt bad.

Here's what happened: I grew up a perfect, good girl. I did everything everyone told me I was supposed to do: picked a good career, went to college for two degrees, found a great guy, got married, had a couple kids, bought a house, got a better-paying job, got promoted, increased my retirement funds, made sure my kids had a college fund, and made sure my husband was happy. And then I proceeded to completely burn out. I was sick more than half a dozen times a year. I spent more time on antibiotics than I care to admit. I suffered the guilt of calling in sick, which then made me sicker. I went to work sick a lot.

I was sick so many times the year after my daughter was born that I started dreading going to work. My days became habitual and zombie-like with a feeling of low-level resentment that would often butt heads with my *I-love-what-I-do* thing. I love helping people. But I was exhausted helping everyone else but me.

"I can't come in today," I'd leave the message on my boss's answering machine, coughing a little more for effect. And the guilt would burn a hole in me the whole time. I knew what the other therapists would have to do to pick up my slack. I hated being the one they'd think of when they were exhausted at the end of their day.

Thing is, I'd really be sick. I wasn't faking it. I was actually a germ-ridden, hacking, feverish mess. And sometimes I'd go to work like that, praying not to sneeze while I was treating someone. My belief was that you showed up, no matter how you felt, because you couldn't let anyone down. That didn't last long. Feeling this way made me miserable, on top of already feeling miserable. I didn't know how to take care of myself or prioritize my own health.

"I can't go in today," I'd complain to my then-husband. "I feel like crap."

"How many sick days do you have?" He'd probe.

"I'm out, but I just can't do it," I'd tell him with a mild nausea starting to form because I could feel his disappointment in me.

Who was I if I was sick? Nobody. A failure. A disappointment. And definitely not a contributor to the family income. It was excruciating to be me when I wasn't feeling well. I was so afraid of disappointing people; I'd rather please them than feel well.

I started pursuing more healing for myself. I started exploring how to feel better and, in doing so, opened up a connection to my soul that I could actually hear for once. Problem was that I was terrified of what she was saying. I'd hear things like, *you're in the wrong job,* and *you're in the wrong marriage,* voices that would require a lot of courage to listen to. Courage I didn't have for the longest time. I was content with my perfect life, even when I started having chest pains that should have served as a wake-up call. I learned how to listen to my body. And she was screaming. But I was really good at ignoring those screams at first.

The purpose-driven fear I began to feel started to move and drive me. I felt it in my gut, my solar plexus, my chest, and my throat. I learned to recognize tightness in these areas and knew I had to do something before it became more painful. I learned to recognize the fear as "excitement without the breath," like my breath worker Lauren explained to me.

Purpose-driven fear was always related to something I wanted to say or do that made me feel more alive and more me, but that also made me feel terrified. It felt exactly like the survival kind of fear, but not the walking-in-a-dark-alley-alone type. It was the feeling that my soul was being squashed, and I'd better take some action before it suffocated to death.

Purpose-driven fear had a feeling of healthy urgency. A bigger-than-me sense of knowing. And it kept up the message until I listened. It wouldn't let me off the hook until I took some kind of action that pointed toward joy. Joy was the relief, every time. Joy was the healer. Joy became a magical elixir, but it would be a while before I figured that out.

It seemed like my entire world became about purpose-driven fear.

And I decided this label of fear needed reframing. I realized if this was going to be a daily practice, I'd have to learn some new skills to be able to deal with it and not have a heart attack.

If you've read my book, *Brave Healing: A Guide for Your Journey*, you know that the fear of speaking up in my marriage was something I'd lived with and finally overcame. What I realized later, after I was on the other side of that mess, is that I had to overcome the thing I didn't think I could do to be able to do all the other things that followed that I really wanted to do. Really awesome, big things. Things that would help me to become the truest, most badass me.

What I had to speak up about first and foremost was what I needed to feel healthy and happy. In the beginning of my marriage, my business goals and dreams were tainted by the shared should's and supposed to's we had come up with, the rules we'd created together as a couple. The problem? I wasn't much of a contributor to those ground rules. I was standing by listening to what my husband thought should happen and reluctantly agreeing most of the time.

I often heard him say, "That's not how business is done!" I was never able to say, "But I want to do it differently." What I heard myself saying over and over again was, "Okay." Even though none of it was okay. Even though I knew in my gut and soul that my way was right for me, even if it went against everything everybody usually did.

When I started getting sick all the time and my days were plagued with anxiety about going to work sick, I knew something had to change, but I was afraid to tell my husband I didn't want to work as many hours. I was afraid to make a change from the plans we'd discussed and agreed upon, because I knew he'd disagree or resist. I knew I'd start up one more battle and more of our already-infrequent hours together would be spent arguing. That didn't seem right. *This isn't what a good marriage should look like,* went through my head a lot.

So instead of taking care of myself, I worked more. I followed the rules and did what I thought I was supposed to do to make things work. I made my business income my goal until achieving that became impossible, until I started to have chest pain and my intuition began speaking to me in ways I couldn't ignore.

I'm asking you now, badass reader, are you listening to your own soul? Where is purpose-driven fear showing up? And a few more questions below you might just spend a few deep breaths with. (Got your notebook?)

Are you a recovering good girl too?

What have you done in the name of that perfect, good girl?

What pieces of yourself do you sacrifice to make others happy?

When was the last time you really thought about what you truly desire? Like really, truly, fully, selfishly want for your life?

How is your body talking to you?

Are you listening to those messages?

Can you get still long enough to listen to the whispers before they become screams?

What messages have you been ignoring?

What do you already know you need to do or say to feel healthier?

What messages are you ignoring, stuffing, distracting yourself from, or numbing up to?

Purpose-driven fear drives you out of your comfort zone for the benefit of your own health and happiness. Purpose-driven fear is there to save your soul and your life. It's meant to help you. It's meant to be a compass pointing you exactly in the direction you need to go in order to do what will most help you achieve your dreams and goals.

And that's why we can have a little more fun with it!

Sometimes the goal is to just feel happy. Sometimes it's to be healthy. The nagging fears you have about these basic needs are some of the purpose-driven kind, because whatever your purpose in this world is, it can't be fulfilled if you're exhausted, sick, or angry all the time. Purpose needs a healthy mind-body to be fulfilled through. It needs a higher vibe kind of energy.

Where can you recognize some of this purpose-driven kind of fear showing up in your life?

How do you know it's this kind versus the "real" kind of fear (the kind that keeps you safe from physical harm)?

What does it feel like?

Start to question these feelings, and begin to journal about what you find.

I owe much of my current fear-crushing ability to my own healers, the people who helped me through the feelings, validated and honored them, encouraged me to feel them, and then helped me use tools to release them. It's good to have guides. They see what you can't. They feel what you're resisting. They help you shift the energy from stuck to flowing. They help guide you to your own awareness and healing power.

I also owe much of my current courage to the writing and speaking teachers and coaches who helped me heal with words on the page and spoken out loud. Healing is in the writing and speaking, and it's in the receiving. Profound healing can hide in the seemingly smallest moment of a few validating or acknowledging words someone speaks to you that help you know you're not alone and open up a little crevice of your heart to be healed..

If you've chosen this healing journey like I have, then you know this work tends to come in layers. We peel each one off and move a little closer to our truest, most authentic self and essence, a feeling that is best described as love. That gains momentum after a while.

Recognizing purpose-driven fear was a feat and a process. And I know there will be no final destination called "fearless." I also know that the journey is about being able to respond in the moment in the way that best serves me; that feels good for my soul; that nourishes my purpose, mission, and calling in the world; and that helps me generously take care of myself and those I love.

Getting to this point required disciplined awareness of body and mind, indomitable spirit, and an unapologetic positive attitude of self-love and compassion. My healers and teachers could only guide me to the next best answer or step. I had to be awake enough to see it and brave enough to take the step. I encourage you to listen to yours without judgment.

I also had to realize that once on the journey, I couldn't really go back. Once you have the awareness, you have no excuses. You can and should take full responsibility for your path. The awareness leads to massive motivation for accountability, which is truly the answer to the billion-dollar question: how do you get people to do what they already know they should do?

The bigger challenge on the journey is that once you've taken those first steps, it's almost guaranteed that things are about to get more interesting and some days even more challenging.

That's not fair! I thought while talking to myself one day about this. I'd crashed really hard into *I'm not good enough* thoughts after a huge success. I was ready to move to a shack on the beach and sell coconuts. I'd had it with awareness and fear and everything else spiritual or good in this world. I wanted to be unconscious again. Seriously, I was done.

Only I woke up the next day ready to try again. *Fuck, here we go again*, I thought.

And that's the warrior's path. Indomitable spirit. It's something my teacher, Master Holloway, taught me in my first few Tae Kwon Do classes. You just don't give up. And that's who you are. That's who you were born to be.

I have a few more questions for you now:

Are you awake for the stuff of your life?

Are you catching yourself when you fall unconscious again?

Are you brave enough to take the next best step, even when you're afraid?

What if this could be easy?

What else is possible?

What if there's something you haven't learned yet that could change everything?

Things are about to get way more fun now. The first thing you're going to need to do is know what you want and why you want it. Let's get this party started and practice by following the enthusiasm of our own desires. Go ahead and give yourself permission to be turned on by life and the dreams you have for it. Like, *really* turned on.

CHAPTER 2

Follow the Enthusiasm of Your Deepest Desires

We're going to start with desire. But I love the word enthusiasm as far as something to go for too. It's a bit stronger than desire. And what about ecstasy? Has it been a while since you thought about feeing ecstatic? Can you remember ever feeling that way? Or were you hushed as a child when that energy bubbled up?

At one point after my divorce, I was standing motionless, staring at the clothes in my closet. Nothing I owned felt like me anymore. I fingered through the collection of tan khaki pants and Easter-egg-colored Polo shirts and wanted to gag. I started ripping everything off the hangers one by one and stuffing them into huge green garbage bags. It was interesting how letting go of the old me, in terms of clothing, felt incredibly liberating.

"OMG, it's about time!" My best friend said to me when I showed up for a lunch date wearing skinny jeans and a t-shirt with a v-neckline a bit lower than she'd seen me wear before.

"I feel like me again," I told her. "I feel sexy. I want to feel like this for the rest of my life."

"This is the real you," she acknowledged what I felt. "This is the you I've known has been there."

Can you remember the last time you felt ecstatic about the way you looked in your clothes? Felt in your body? If the answer is no, it's because you were most likely taught not to. I don't ever remember being given permission to be overflowing with enthusiasm or ecstasy. I mostly remember being told to "hush." In school, at home, at soccer practice, in college, at work meetings, and by my ex. For much of my life, I remember being told to behave, and that meant being quiet, appropriate, professional. Being quiet meant that I cared, or that I was being good.

In fact, many times in those environments there were not-so-good consequences for expressing like that. So the little me started off her life with a fear of what would happen if I was too much, too loud, inappropriate, or otherwise a bad girl. I equated speaking up with being bad or having a bad consequence. You can guess the rest of that story. I spent at least two decades recovering from this, finding my voice, and using it for the benefit of my health and delivering the gifts I was born to deliver.

Passion, desire, enthusiasm, and ecstasy are big feelings with a lot of positive manifesting energy. To honor those bad (good) girls, we would need to be in full-on, unapologetic expression of that big energy, in all ways; speaking, being, dressing, working, loving, etc.

Sadly, most of us were taught to suppress that stuff. And even sadder is the fact that many of us became perfect at suppressing it, along with our truest selves and biggest gifts in the process. Many of us have had jobs where the dress code stifles us. We've had to follow rules about how we act, dress, speak, and perform since we were kids. Some of us are still doing that. Some of us will die doing that.

More questions for you. Got your notebook?

Were you conditioned right out of your own desire?

Have you given your truest desires any thought for a while? Or *ever*?

Are you still in fear of what the consequences might be if you express yourself in these ways?

It's time to connect with your desire. And this step is so key to this book that if you skip this chapter, don't expect to have any fun with your fear. Do you see the link between them?

Some of the desire talk here is thanks to Esther Hicks and her Law of Attraction teachings. When I started down that path fifteen or twenty years ago, it was via the book *The Secret*. I learned about Esther Hicks later on, and her ability to express and teach the Law of Attraction has fascinated me ever since. As she says, step one is desire. And we're wired for it. To not want would be alien.

It took me a while to go after the desire because I hadn't done the healing work necessary to uncover the layers suffocating my desires. There was so much of what other people (parents, teachers, coaches, friends, family members, bosses, spouse, kids) told me I should want, I fell out of touch with my own true desires. I had no idea what felt good to me. I lived through duty and obligation.

This is why the Law of Attraction won't work in some cases. You're moving toward desires that aren't yours. You're moving toward what you think you want. And the proof is that usually when you achieve those things, you still don't feel good. In fact, if you had paid close enough attention, your body may have been giving you the clues all along. You were just good at ignoring them. I know I was.

I'm pretty sure I made it through my undergrad studies, grad school, my first two or three jobs, and a twenty-year marriage before I actually clued in to the fact that what I thought I wanted actually didn't always feel great.

The desire has to be yours. The way you know it's yours is that it feels good. Really good. Ecstatic, even. And to use your desire as a first step to moving through purpose-driven fear, the desires have to be big.

We're about to practice all of this.

The desire has to burn brightly enough inside you to overpower everything else. If you aren't able to connect with that kind of feeling, then you might have to practice this step for a while. Know that you have the power to feel into this in any moment. When you are aware, you take responsibility for how and what you feel, and you get to choose.

Are you familiar with Danielle LaPorte's Desire Map? That would be an excellent adjunct to this chapter. She'll get you diving into how you want to feel, and that's right where we need to go to have the most fun with fear. I loved her book, *The Fire Starter Sessions*, and had a great time learning my core desired feelings.

Fear is a feeling. Desires also have a feeling. When you know how you want to feel, and you can conjure that up instantly, you begin to understand how to use fear and how to have more fun with it. You learn how to shift fear into fuel for your desires. That's badass. That's a ninja move on fear.

Every time you experience fear of something that aligns with purpose, you have an opportunity to move toward that purpose. If you understand feeling as the language of all of this, you'll have one of the biggest secrets to life. You will never feel freer than the moment you take responsibility for this one thing: your own joy and desire. When you make every moment a small, aware move toward joy, your daily moments become that. Your life becomes that.

And the way you do that is by feeling what turns you on to the point of unbridled enthusiasm. Or how about some illegal amounts of joy? Pure ecstasy sound fun? Do you have any idea what that even means for yourself?

I started experimenting with new experiences during the time I was separated from my husband and ready to have some fun.

"Do you want to go to Soundcheck with us this weekend?" My girlfriend asked me one day to go to a nightclub where they were having a rave. I'd never explored this as a twenty-something. I was too afraid of what might happen.

"Totally!" I replied.

The night of my first rave was like opening a door to a candy store, only inside was the best music you've ever heard, the highest-vibe crowd of strangers you've ever met, and the most fun you've ever had. I'd found a new joy. Raving and writing would help me get through my separation and divorce.

It's going to be worth the experiment—this joy thing. And truly, if you die having known this one thing about yourself—what really turns you on—wouldn't that be enough?

Answer a few more questions for me:

What do you really, truly, selfishly desire?

How do you really want to feel?

Can you conjure up that feeling right this moment? Go for it; give it a try.

What do you have to give yourself permission to feel?

What feelings have you been told are bad?

Time to think and believe something better, healthier, and more badass now.

Let's do an amazing exercise to get you connected with your feeling senses and in tune with the language of your desire, your soul, and your intuition. Grab your notebook, pen, and a timer, and have them handy.

But first, a quick note about the exercises in this book.

Every time I guide you to feel and write, know it's the combination of the two that makes this book and the Brave Healing method work. If you skip the body awareness stuff, you'll be skipping the most important and powerful part of the work. If you skip the writing, you'll also be skipping the most powerful, important part of the work. If you don't do the two together, you may just be cheating yourself out of a true shift or transformation.

When you're ready to do the exercises in this book, make sure you have enough time to do them in their entirety, both the body awareness piece and the writing piece together. As you move through the book and practice these exercises, they'll become easier and more natural, and you'll find yourself connected to a much more powerful place for all your thinking, writing, and expressing.

What you'll need for the exercises: A notebook or piece of paper, a pen, and a timer.

Guidelines for the writing: Stay centered in your body and practice noticing how you feel. Connect to the breath and the sensations of it. Move the words from inside of you to the paper. Don't censor yourself. Write as fast as you can. Don't worry about spelling, punctuation, grammar, or finishing sentences. No rules, just write. If for any reason you can't write or type, then you can speak and record your words that way. The important part is the expression.

If you find yourself in a mindset of doubt or fear, or you begin to feel some resistance in you, it's all good. Use that awareness to take the next breath and write the next word. It's the process that matters, and anything that occurs in your own process is part of the magic. So pay attention, especially to your own resistance.

What might get you stuck: In the beginning, you'll start to differentiate the inner critic voice from the intuitional voice. Each has a feeling, a flow, and a quality. If your writing feels stuck, it's most likely because you've checked out of your feeling body and you're back into the dark alley of your mind again, facing those inner critic messages.

Notice when this happens. Take another grounding, centering breath, and then allow what's coming through to flow to the page without getting in your own way. Your judgement of your writing and what it should look like is what stops you up. What you're making the feelings mean stops you up even more. Don't add baggage to your baggage.

For the purpose of moving through fear, we first must be able to feel and become masters of that feeling domain in ourselves. It takes some practice. With practice, you'll notice some momentum. And with that momentum, you'll notice a feeling of freedom emerge. When you're feeling freedom around fear, things get pretty darn fun.

Exercise 1: Give yourself permission to desire

Body Awareness Exercise: Find a comfortable place to sit or lie down. If you'd like to listen to a recorded version of this exercise, you'll find that here: https://lauradifranco.com/brave-book-resources/.

Close your eyes and start to connect with your breathing. Clear your mind and anchor into the senses. What do you feel? What sensations do you notice?

Relax your body, unclenching and releasing the weight of your body into the chair or bed. With every exhale, soften, release, relax, and let go a little more.

Relax your head, neck, throat, and shoulders. Soften the space behind your eyes, through your jaw, and down through your throat and neck.

As thoughts come, release them and reconnect with the sensations of your body and breath. Relax and soften your chest, upper back, and torso, releasing all the way to your fingertips.

With every exhale, allow your body to get heavier and relax. Allow your low back, belly, hips, buttocks, and thighs to soften.

Continue to clear your mind and notice the sensations of your body instead. What do you notice? Relax and release your legs, knees, and feet. Feel your feet on the floor, the surface of your body on the chair, the clothes on your body, the temperature in the room . . . or whatever other sensation comes into your awareness. Relax and breathe like this for several more minutes.

Take a couple final deep breaths and slowly open your eyes. Move directly into the writing exercise without a break.

Write it: Set your timer for five minutes and fill in the blank. What I really desire right now is _____.

When you're finished writing, take a few breaths and identify how you feel within your body. Notice how embodied you feel. Did the writing pull you back out of your feeling senses into your thoughts? What do you feel right now?

Speak it: Next, you're going to read your piece out loud to yourself.

Don't underestimate the power of this part of the exercise. Putting the vibration of your voice to the soul-driven words you just wrote is going to help make them real. Take a moment now to read your piece out loud to yourself.

What do you feel now? Check in with your body. Notice what's going on. And if you have time, you can write a little bit more about what you feel or on the writing prompt itself.

Exercise 2: Determine What Joy Feels Like

This exercise will help you start to understand the language of your own intuition and inner healer and wisdom. That language is a felt sense in your body. Joy has a physical feeling, and things that are the opposite of joy have a different physical feeling.

In this exercise, you're going to develop a cheat sheet of sorts to help you differentiate those two ways of feeling so that you can start moving yourself toward what feels good—what feels like joy—and the things you truly desire.

To begin, draw a line vertically down the middle of a regular piece of paper or a journal page so that you make two columns. On the left side, put the title "Hell No" at the top, and on the right side, put the title "Hell Yes."

Starting on the left, set a timer for five minutes and make a list of how the "Hell No's" feel in your body. This would be something that feels like the opposite of joy. If you're not sure, think about something you know you don't want and see how it feels. For example, when I'm feeling something that's no good for me, it will show up as chest tightness or a choky feeling in my throat.

The "Hell No!" is sometimes about something to which I've said yes, but meant no. It's something that does not nourish me or bring me joy. It does not energize or assist me. It tends to do the opposite. I'm sure you can find plenty of examples in your own life. Use those to make your list of the ways this feels, literally, in your physical body. Describe it as many ways as you can think of.

The "Hell Yes!" reaction has a good, nourishing, energizing, and freeing feeling in the body. I notice that it assists me, supports me, and lets me know joy is here. A yes brings me joy. It has a physical feeling in me. For example, when things are a "Hell Yes!" for me, I feel strong, weightless, and free.

Okay, now go make your list. Set your timer for five minutes and do the right side of the page, the "Hell Yes"es. Write as many descriptive words as you can think of for how those feel in your body. Describe the way the yes, or joy, feels in you as many ways as you can think of.

When you're done, look at the columns. You now have a pretty good cheat sheet about when your soul is feeling a "Yes" or a "No." And it's time to start asking yourself how many times you say yes when your body is telling you no.

When do you compromise a small piece of yourself by doing things that don't feel good?

When in the past have you moved toward something that was clearly a no?

It's time to begin following your desire, joy, and enthusiasm. And that shows up in your body. Desires, dreams, goals, purpose, mission, and calling have an excited "Hell Yes!" to them. You can begin to practice how this feels in you and master it.

The real mastery comes when you're following the desire more often than moving against it. When you're tilting your teeter totter toward the joy side.

I had one student ask me during this exercise, "What if I don't know how something feels, or I feel confused?"

"That's a no," I told her. Because when something is fuzzy, foggy, confusing, or you're not sure how you feel, it's for sure not a "Hell Yes!"

So be clear next time, when you're feeling confused and having trouble making that decision, it's usually because it's not a yes. When you start to know the feelings in your body, you're going to have an incredibly powerful internal GPS system, one that is constantly telling you exactly how to move toward your truest, deepest desires. You've always had that. It's just a matter of getting in touch with it again.

Here's the thing about desire: purpose-driven fear will show up in moments you step out of your comfort zone and move toward your deepest desires, especially if you're not used to going for things you want, have been taught not to follow your heart, or have been a bit resigned to the content, safe life you've been living.

Everything must start with authentic, soul-driven, core desires.

Knowing what those are and how they feel inside you is the way you'll not only recognize purpose-driven fear but begin to act with it and have more fun when it shows up.

Lastly, be a warrior about your own desires. Meaning, start to practice voicing them, writing them down, speaking about them and taking action toward them, unapologetically. Prioritizing your deepest desires and joy creates the energy you then get to serve others with. It provides the overflow from which you can give and serve.

Being selfish about your own desires and joys is what creates the energy you'll need to help others. Self-care, including living for your own joy on a regular basis, is a necessity, not a luxury. And if you're aiming to change the world, you'll have to master this before serving others starts to feel easy, like what you were born for.

Now let's explore what you were born for and the why behind what you do now. The why needs to be big enough to make you cry.

CHAPTER 3

Your Why Should Make You Cry

When I first heard the statement that your why should make you cry, I understood what it meant. When I first *felt* the true meaning of those words, my soul opened up and tears slid down my cheeks as I felt the reason I was born moving through me. It was that good.

I'd just started teaching at The Writers Center in Maryland and my workshop, *Writing as a Path to Healing*, was a new addition to their usual technical writing docket. I was honored to be there, bringing this work to the world.

I floated out of the forty-year-old building on the corner of Walsh Street and Rockville Pike looking up at the clear, night sky and smiling. I'd just taught my first live workshop to fifteen engaged, kind, aware, and heart-centered writers. A summer breeze met my face as I quickly crossed the street to my car, pulled the door shut, and dialed my mom's phone number.

"Hey Mom! I just finished the workshop," I got the words out and listened to the reply I already knew was coming, "Oh, how did it go, honey?"

"Mom, I think I was born for this!" I choked out and then pivoted the microphone end of my iPhone toward the roof so she couldn't hear me start to sob.

"Honey?! Are you okay?" She replied while I continued getting myself together enough to actually speak more words.

"I'm good," I cried. She let me cry for another few seconds before speaking more motherly things. "Oh honey, I know. I'm so happy for you. I'm so proud of you." It doesn't matter how old you are—you're always your parents' baby.

That moment brought me back to other major junctures in my life and had me remembering how they'd felt. I was stoked on my sixteenth birthday when I brought my first car home, having paid for it with my pizza-making money. I felt super proud walking across the stage to receive my diplomas in undergrad and grad school. I was overjoyed to get the yes from my first employer at a big hospital. I was excited and joyful on my wedding day, and when we brought our first dog home, my smile was huge.

When my son was born, I felt awed and humbled by life and the sheer miracle lying on my chest. When my daughter was born, the same intense feelings graced my heart. When I opened my own business, the freedom flowing to my soul was amazing. When my kids laughed and told me stories about their day, I marveled, so enthralled by their moment of joy, I felt like it was my own.

When I received my first check for a published article in *Tae Kwon Do Times* magazine, you couldn't have wiped the grin off my face for nothin'. Standing by my son's side as we earned our black belts together after six years of training? Well . . . I don't know who I was more happy for, me or him.

When readers emailed, "You changed my life," that got really close to pure joy. I felt I was playing that game, Hot and Cold, and getting much warmer. Something tingled inside. I knew the work I'd done about purpose, mission, and calling was paying off. I was happy more days than not. It was a better feeling than the drug of achievement.

When I asked for my divorce, relief, freedom, and happiness spread through me like wildfire. A necessary choice to ready me for what was next. Along with that hardest year of my life came reclaiming my worth—a jump toward happiness I'd never lose again.

But the night I finished teaching those fifteen amazing souls, after sitting there sharing my stories of worth, and truth, and healing and watching as they absorbed my enthusiasm, listened with bright, hopeful eyes, and then, with huge amounts of courage, shared their own stories and helped others release their tears . . . that night was the bomb of happiness for me.

I knew in that moment I was born for it: for healing, for teaching, and for inspiring others to live fiercely alive.

The day I knew my purpose, claimed my mission, and listened to my calling, without doubting it, wondering if I deserved it, being afraid to go after it, or comparing it to others . . . that day I knew my whole life had changed for the better.

That day was the happiest, most amazing day of my life. I've carried that lasting joy with me since, giving myself permission to use the inspiration, positivity, energy, and fire of it to light my moments and keep me on point with everything I do. That joy has stamina no other moment or event has ever had.

That joy was real, unexpected, and true. That kind of joy's got the power to change the world. And the night I accepted it into my heart, allowed myself to feel it down into my bones, and then let it burst out in tears to my mom on the phone was the moment I felt a bigger thing driving my bus. For once, I knew I could surrender and go for the ride.

"I love you, Mom," I said. "I'll let you know how next week goes."

"Great, honey, I can't wait to hear!" she said, and I let the rest of the tears fall on my way home as I finished letting bliss take me over and have its way with me. *So this's what that feels like*, I thought and smiled. I looked, blurry-eyed, up to the moon one last time and whispered, "Thank you."

I had not just found but *felt* my big why. The why, while it takes many shapes over the years of one's life, has a steady and consistent feel. And it's the feeling I want you to go for. The sometimes indescribable feeling of joy and purpose mixed together is what I'm talking about. And only you can feel your version of it.

Now it's your turn, amazing, brave reader. Time to go for the joy.

Time to put yourself and your dreams up front, at the top of your list, and go after them with a crazy kind of determination, awareness, and love. Time to treat yourself and your purpose like the golden nuggets they are. Time to change the world with your gifts.

Feeling your why is more important than you think if you're really ready to have fun with your fear. You must explore your why, and you must explore it deep enough to find the feeling underneath. And then you must feel the feeling before you have the condition for it, like believing it before you see it. Because it is this feeling of pure joy mixed with purpose that fuels everything else to follow. Joy *is* your purpose.

Being able to conjure up and remember your why is what gets you through your purpose-driven fear. It's what you'll flip your switch to when you remember. And it's what starts to make feeling that purpose-driven fear more fun. You'll always have the idea of the feeling that sits just on the other side of that fear. And that feeling . . . oh, that amazing feeling. It's worth going for.

And I have a secret for you. Everything you desire is *not* sitting on the other side of fear. It's claimed on your way through it, the very second you take the action with that feeling inside you. All you really need to do is move, act, breathe, speak . . . armed with the feeling of purpose-driven fear, fueled by the joy and purpose of your why.

Let's do another exercise to solidify this.

What you'll need for the exercise: A notebook or piece of paper, a pen, and a timer.

Guidelines for the writing: Stay centered in your body. Connect to the breath. Move the words from the inside to the paper. Don't censor yourself. Write as fast as you can. Don't worry about spelling, punctuation, grammar, or finishing sentences. No rules, just write.

Exercise 3: Getting to and Feeling Your Big Why

Answer five big, brave questions to help you connect with your soul, listen to the language of your intuition, and get started on the journey to your joy and your why. Begin by quieting down, connecting with your body and breath, and clearing your mind.

Body Awareness Exercise: Find a comfortable place to sit or lie down. If you'd like to listen to a recorded version of this exercise, you'll find that here: https://soundcloud.com/lauraprobert/body-awareness-audio.

Close your eyes and start to connect with your breathing. Clear your mind and anchor into the senses. What do you feel? What sensations do you notice?

Relax your body, unclenching and releasing the weight of your body into the chair or bed. With every exhale, soften, release, relax, and let go a little more.

Relax your head, neck, throat, and shoulders. Soften the space behind your eyes, through your jaw, and down through your throat and neck.

As thoughts come, release them and reconnect with the sensations of your body and breath. Relax and soften your chest, upper back, and torso, releasing all the way to your fingertips.

With every exhale, allow your body to get heavier and let go. Relax and soften your low back, belly, hips, buttocks, and thighs. Continue to clear your mind and notice the sensations of your body instead. What do you notice?

Relax and release your legs, knees, and feet. Feel your feet on the floor, the surface of your body on the chair, the clothes on your body, the temperature in the room . . . or whatever other sensation comes into your awareness.

Relax and breathe like this for several more minutes. Take a couple final deep breaths and slowly open your eyes. Move directly into the writing exercise without a break.

Write it: When you're ready, set your timer for five minutes and write as fast as you can until the timer goes off. Do that for each of these questions. Ready to write? Grab your notebook and pen and ask yourself:

1. What if there were nobody left to offend, upset, or disappoint? Who would I become?

2. What do I need to give myself permission to think, say, do or have?

3. Where in my life am I not living in integrity with my own intuition, soul, and deepest desires?

4. What do I love to do so much I lose track of time?

5. When am I filled up with so much gratitude, it overwhelms me?

Speak it: As a bonus challenge, read your answers to someone you love and trust afterward, putting your own voice to the words.

Let's talk about what's behind these questions now that you've had a chance to answer them.

CARING ABOUT WHAT OTHER PEOPLE THINK

Thing is, we all come at life from our own perspective and filters, depending on how we grew up and what our influences have been. Caring about what other people think limits you to their perspective only. It means you're following rules other people gave you, rather than living on your own terms and listening to your own intuition. We'll tackle this specific fear in a later chapter in a much more detailed way. For now, just think about how this shows up in your life and make some notes about that. Your big why must come from you, not from what others have told you is good for you.

HAVING PERMISSION TO BE YOURSELF

We grow up listening to parents, teachers, and coaches and live by the rules we're taught. When we grow up and start playing in the big, bad world, we sometimes are still living by those same rules, even though they may not serve us or our dreams anymore. It's good to use awareness to understand what beliefs are limiting you now. And it might be time to make a change or two! Who are you waiting for to give you permission to be yourself? Don't you think it's time to give yourself permission? To live your big why, you must give yourself permission to feel it and go for it. Nobody else can do that for you. Permission granted to be selfish about this. It's your life. You decide.

BEING IN ALIGNMENT WITH YOUR INTUITION

This is a feel thing. How many times do you say "yes" when you mean "no?" How many times are you feeling that something isn't right for you, but because you're following the should's and supposed to's, you say yes anyway? Being in alignment means you're listening to the messages and following what nourishes you, not what depletes you. Think about where this shows up in your life and make some notes. You might want to go back to your cheat sheet and add some more descriptive words to your lists. Make sure to have that list handy when you need it. Your intuition is what leads you to your big why. You need a strong trust and faith in it as well as a strong connection to it. Intuition is the language of your soul, the messages that come through about your purpose, joy, and why.

FOLLOWING WHAT YOU LOVE

There's magic in following the pull of your desire, passion, and loves. I use gratitude and love as my go-to's. When you're following the things you love and doing them more and more, the energy with which you're living begins to help you attract more of what you love. This is the Law of Attraction. One of my biggest influences in this arena is Esther Hicks. Make sure you find her *PureJOY* channel on YouTube. The things you love ignite joy. And because joy is your purpose, you must feel and follow the joy. Love and joy lead you to your purpose and your why.

USING THE ENERGY OF GRATITUDE

Similarly, when you choose gratitude in any circumstance, you're choosing your own thoughts, beliefs, and actions, rather than allowing the circumstances of your life to control you and let you spiral down into negativity. With awareness, you have the choice to pick something that feels good, something you're grateful for, in any moment. I find the energy of gratitude and appreciation to be incredibly helpful when I can't find anything else to flip my switch to. And it's one of the energies we'll explore when we have fun with our purpose-driven fear. It's a fear-buster! Gratitude, along with love and joy, are bridges to your purpose and why. In fact, gratitude and fear cannot exist in the brain at the same time. Pick gratitude!

These questions, along with many more, along with some deep inner healing work and the love and support of people like Mom, have catapulted me into my purpose, and there's no going back.

BUST THROUGH FEAR TO JOY

There's no sugarcoating it: your fear will paralyze you at first. But when you jump through that wall of fire, get to the other side, and look back to realize it was only a millimeter thick, you'll begin to feel the unstoppable feeling of joy drive everything you do.

You'll find the courage to jump by knowing your own deepest desires and joys, along with the why behind them, and by strengthening the muscles of love and gratitude. These practices can be mastered to the point of them being the lighthouse that guides you every step of the way, even when the storms come. They are your compass for having more fun with your fear.

Cheers to your courage! You're building those muscles and mastering the awareness that will take you to the next step.

Exercise 4: Claim Your Big Why

Now let's claim our big why! Get out your notebook and pen and spend as much time as you need with this. Why are you doing what you're doing? Why do you want what you want? What is the feeling behind the desire? Why is it so important to you? One thing to pay attention to is your own resistance during the writing. What's coming up? Don't get stuck here; just let the words flow.

Answer the question: My big why is _____.

Now you're armed with one of the most important weapons against fear: the why behind your desires. But to truly reframe fear to a feeling you can have fun with, you're going to need a more powerful weapon in your toolkit: consistently conscious, positive thoughts. Let's get to it! And bring that big, badass why with you!

CHAPTER 4

Don't Believe
Everything You Think

Nobody will ever want what you have to offer, at least not enough for you to make a living. That's what I thought to myself. I also believed, *You're never going to be as good as* (fill in the blank with whomever you envy).

I could go on with some of my nastier inner dialogue (*you're stupid* comes to mind), but it would be a waste of our time in this important and powerful chapter. It's time to shut that shit down and think something better for a change. T. Harv Eker taught me not to believe any of the old, conditioned, or negative thoughts I think. And it's working.

This is the tool that'll change your game. This is the tool that you'll use, on top of a foundation of badass awareness, that'll create everything you desire. You create what you think. Notice your thoughts lately?

How intensely do you believe what you think? Do you want to be right? Or would you rather be happy? Remember that question from Dr. Phil? I loved it and repeat it to myself when I'm in the middle of any kind of disagreement. I've also learned a tool from one of my favorite mentors,

Brené Brown, who reminds us to ask, "What's the story I'm telling myself about this?"

If you haven't watched her TED talk on vulnerability or her latest Netflix special, *Call to Courage*, please go do that. They're going to help you with your awareness game.

I want you to pay particular attention to your inner voice during this chapter. Slow down a bit so you can feel your own resistance and hear your own messages as you read and reflect. Take a few breaths in between sentences. Be super curious; be your own detective. Go on a mission to know everything about how and why you think what you think. If you've practiced this work before, I challenge you to go deeper. Go slower. Really feel into another layer. Watch the movie of your mind's thoughts. "I know that already," is one of the biggest ways you'll get in the way of taking everything to the next level, so be open to exploring even those aspects you think you've got a handle on.

Whatever you think is your truth. This piece is so important that my heart is beating a little more quickly in my chest as I'm sitting here writing it. *They have to get this part,* I'm thinking. *They have to know how powerful this is.*

Think about that for a moment. What have you been creating for yourself up until now? What thoughts dominate your mind on a regular basis? Now think about something better, healthier, and more aligned with your desires and goals. It's as hard or as easy as you think it'll be. Why not choose easy?

Let's do a powerful exercise to get you right into the act of transforming your fear into fuel for your dreams. I'll talk about the difference between survival and purpose-driven fear, the kinds of purpose-driven fear, and the toolkit you'll need in later chapters. For now, consider this book a workbook, and go grab your notebook and pen again.

If you're a fan of books like *The Secret,* or people like Esther Hicks, and you're on board with positive thinking, forget that for now because there's something better. It's *feeling* you should be interested in. And I've been priming you for that in the last few chapters.

Because the transformative power behind having more fun with fear and living a life that feels courageous and joyful is conjuring up a powerful, purposeful, awesome feeling with the thought you're having. This is a choice you have at any moment of your day, with every breath you take. That's 23,040 opportunities per day. With awareness, you get the choice. And as scary as that sounds, you'll find true freedom in taking responsibility for how you feel (everything you feel) as soon as you begin to practice this.

To get to the feeling, we have to sort through a lot of thoughts and beliefs. They're sticky suckers. Our conditioned thoughts make us feel comfortable and safe in our zone. But those habitual thoughts and beliefs are keeping us stuck, paralyzed, and miserable. They keep us playing small, and they are not helpful or useful anymore.

As Esther says, "A belief is just a thought you keep thinking."

What are some of your own limiting beliefs? What thoughts do you actually believe?

Weird questions, huh? Like, if you knew what they were, you'd stop thinking them, right? Well, how's that working for you? If you're like me, you have some awareness, and you still catch yourself in the act. Especially when you're afraid.

Stop believing everything you think when you're afraid. And when you do, notice how tired you are of your own bullshit. Notice the habitual tape that plays. And choose something new. Anything will be better than the old stuff. If you can't find a better thought, then just breathe. Clear your mind and go neutral for a few breaths. Meditate a little.

Fear keeps you standing still, mouth shut, powerless and unworthy. You've let that fear keep you there until now. Now it's time to think, believe, and act differently. Get curious. Question everything. The beginning of awareness is learning to question everything you think is right and true about your life.

Just a quick reminder: every time I guide you to feel and write, know it's the combination of the two that makes this method work. If you skip the body awareness stuff, you'll be skipping the most important and powerful part of the work. If you skip the writing, you'll also be skipping the most powerful, important part of the work. If you don't do the two together, you may just be cheating yourself out of a true shift or transformation.

What you'll need for the exercise: A notebook or piece of paper, a pen, and a timer.

Guidelines for the writing: Stay centered in your body. Connect to the breath. Move the words from the inside to the paper. Don't censor yourself. Write as fast as you can. Don't worry about spelling, punctuation, grammar, or finishing sentences. No rules, just write.

Time for an exercise.

Exercise 5: Recognize Your Inner Critic Voices

Body Awareness Exercise: Find a comfortable place to sit or lie down. If you'd like to listen to a recorded version of this exercise, you'll find that here: https://soundcloud.com/lauraprobert/body-awareness-audio.

Close your eyes and start to connect with your breathing. Clear your mind and anchor into the senses. What do you feel? What sensations do you notice?

Relax your body, unclenching and releasing the weight of your body into the chair or bed. With every exhale, soften, release, relax, and let go a little more. Relax your head, neck, throat, and shoulders. Soften the space behind your eyes, through your jaw, and down through your throat and neck.

As thoughts come, release them and reconnect with the sensations of your body and breath. Relax and soften your chest, upper back, and torso, releasing all the way to your fingertips. With every exhale, allow your body to get heavier and let go. Relax and soften your low back, belly, hips, buttocks, and thighs. Continue to clear your mind and notice the sensations of your body instead. What do you notice?

Relax and release your legs, knees, and feet. Feel your feet on the floor, the surface of your body on the chair, the clothes on your body, the temperature in the room ... or whatever other sensation comes into your awareness. Relax and breathe like this for several more minutes. Take a couple of final deep breaths and slowly open your eyes. Move directly into the writing exercise without a break.

Write it: Set a timer for five minutes. What are the messages in your head, or the voices you hear when you're afraid, doubtful, anxious, ashamed, or not good enough? List as many as you can.

What you think—including thoughts about yourself, the world, your situation, the future, your family/friends/loved ones/co-workers/boss, your possibilities, your expectations, your opinions, what you know for sure, your past, your wounds, etc.—are all tapes that play in your head based on past experiences and hopes for the future. Writing them down is a first step to being aware of them. Recognizing the patterns of self-sabotage is crucial to busting through fear and thinking something healthier.

Speaking: Re-read your list out loud now, and then circle the three worst voices that come up on a regular, repetitive basis. Which ones trigger you the most? Which voices do you find yourself blocked up and paralyzed by most often?

Can you recognize where these voices come from? Was this message something you heard from a parent, teacher, coach, or other influence from when you were younger? Was it a voice you heard later in life from a spouse, family member, counselor, or co-worker? Is it coming from your scared little girl?

This will make you look stupid, I thought. I'd been listening to my ex-husband rant about how my newest poetry book was "not viable," and

I could feel my body shriveling around my solar plexus. *Maybe he's right,* passed through my mind, *maybe this is all a waste of time.*

Getting to know the voices, their origin, and their power over you is important. This is awareness you'll use later when you're laughing at them, having a conversation that goes something like, "Thanks, but I got this."

With awareness of our thoughts comes the choice to pick new ones that better serve our goals. I had to constantly question my own voices. I had to constantly ask myself, *where is that coming from?* When I realized how harsh that inner critic had become, and realized I'd never talk to other people the way I was talking to myself, I laughed out loud.

One powerful tool you can use to battle these kinds of voices in your head is to ask yourself how you'd talk to a young child who was having the same thought. Or how you'd speak to your best friend. Usually it's much kinder than you're speaking to yourself. Usually you're somewhat of a badass when you are helping other people, like the compassion, kindness, and listening factors are off the chain. So why aren't you doing that for yourself?

We're always so much harsher on ourselves. When you imagine saying those things to a small child, you cringe. You'd never do that! So why are you saying those things to yourself? And more importantly, why are you believing them?

When I have the awareness now, the thoughts seem funny. I calm down. I realize, all of a sudden, what power I now have. The moments I wake up are moments I take my power back from the people I give it away to. All of the little moments of awareness are like tiny gifts being given back to my heart and soul, little chunks that had been ripped out when I let people's opinions weigh heavily on my dreams or believed my own voices telling me I would never be good enough. When I stop now and realize what I'm making someone else's opinion mean, I unpack the baggage I'm piling on top of my baggage.

Slowing down the train of thinking feels impossible some days, but it's exactly the thing you'll need to do to have massive amounts of fun with your fear. You'll have to get really good at catching yourself.

Stopping to pause, notice the thoughts, and be curious about them will change your ability to function in the moment of fear. Questioning your thoughts in the moment and using tools to move with the thoughts and feelings will be the shift you're craving. You'll be able to do this more easily with practice.

Whenever you can, slow down and notice what you're thinking, question the belief and whether it feels limiting or not, write it down or speak about it out loud, recognize that it has a physical feeling in your body (we'll have more fun with that in Chapter 5), clear your mind, and breathe with that feeling.

Is the thought on that list of voices you made earlier? Call it out! Recognize it as one of those habitual tapes. Is there a new one you need to add to your list?

Tapping is another tool you can add to your awareness practice here. I learned Emotional Freedom Technique first from Nick Ortner and then through Denise Duffield-Thomas and her *Lucky Bitch Money Bootcamp*. The idea is that the habitual thoughts you have are subconscious, and we need to get to those subconscious thoughts and reprogram them. Tapping is a powerful reprogramming tool. I use this when I'm experiencing an unusually ingrained pattern or voice that won't seem to quit.

All of these tools create more awareness. Awareness is the foundation for courage and joy. The goal of this book is for you to have fun while you're feeling courageous and doing the things that used to make you feel afraid and paralyzed. The goal is to finally feel the feeling of purpose-driven fear, not make it mean anything, take action with it, and then smile on the journey to your dreams.

One way to have fun right now is to realize you're already busting up the old patterns that have created where you are now. You're already on your way to doing this differently. When you gain awareness, you can't really go back. It's only a matter of practicing from here on out. It's only a matter of the strength of your discipline. And those choices are made one at a time, one day at a time.

One of the most important things we'll need to practice now is feeling—the foundation of all awareness. So we're headed back into the body to feel. You're used to thinking your way through and listening to the wrong voices (the list you made). The next part of the book is the awareness tool that will change everything when it comes to your purpose-driven fear-busting toolkit.

PART TWO

Mastering the Art of Feeling and Awareness

The next four chapters are going to give you the foundation of mind-body awareness you need to transform your fear from paralyzing to power-filled. We'll explore feeling in terms of observing both mind and body, and how sensing all of it will be necessary for a successful playdate with fear. We'll also begin to differentiate survival fear from purpose-driven fear by using our body as the language of our intuition and inner wisdom.

If Fear Were Just a Feeling

If fear were just a feeling
I'd tell it to go to Hell
"Stop sabotaging my biggest dreams,"
I'd say
"Stop making me feel so small!"

If fear were just a feeling
I'd wake up to this aha
"There you go again,"
I'd say
"You can't take me very far."

I'd recognize how it stops me
I'd realize how useless it is
I'd see the added meaning
I make up in my head
And the power that I give

If I notice fear's a feeling
I'll stand up inside of it
breathe deeply through
the noise it makes
and see it as a gift

I can use my fear
as a guide
let it point me to my dreams
with awareness there's a choice
fear's not what it seems

If fear were just a feeling
it'd have nothing over me
I'd use it as a tool
let it fuel
the me I want to be

Fear is just a feeling
Check in with what you sense
relax
let go into it
it's excitement without the breath

Fear's just a feeling
you can choose
a new way to believe
stay awake to the feeling
and notice what you see

The warrior is waiting
she's ready to take action
get out of her way
let her drive
and feel the satisfaction

You can do anything
you fear
anything you want to do
it's time to bust through your mind
and show us the true you.

CHAPTER 5

Permission to Feel Everything

"Fear is just excitement without the breath."

LAUREN CAFRITZ

Here's where the fun starts: with feeling. Here's where every health professional who studies and writes about fear-busting misses the boat. You can't have fun with your fear unless you recognize that it's a physical feeling in your body and stop making it mean something. And because you've most likely been trained to feel less, not more, we'll have to practice a bit.

Fear is a feeling. When you clear your mind, what's left is a feeling in your body, an actual physical sensation. The problem with the feeling of fear is we make it mean a whole lotta things. The big problem is we think, instead of just feel.

I noticed my feeling of fear big time one night while getting ready to drift off to sleep. I pulled the down comforter up to my chin and my hand slid up around my throat. I noticed it felt like I was choking. There was a knot there. I was afraid. I felt small. I felt three years old. I wanted to say, "I love you." But I couldn't. I was afraid of being rejected. Of not being worthy of love. So I didn't say it. And the knot sat there for a while until I drifted off to sleep.

It's the speaking up that always puts me into a state of fear like this. I recognize it now. I know my three-year-old better today. The warrior woman holds her hand more often and guides her. This happens when I want to express big things, like love. It happens when I need to stand up for myself and disagree with someone. It happens when I'm sharing myself with strangers for the first time. I've learned to feel the feeling, take a deep breath, try not to rehearse my words, and just let them flow.

Based on our childhoods, past experiences with failure, pain, tragedy, or trauma, based on what we've been taught and how we were treated from the time we were very small, we think a lot of things about that feeling of fear. We can even have lingering generational trauma-induced fear within us. We proceed to believe those things for the rest of our lives. Sometimes we'll get to a point in our adult lives when it feels like something needs to change. Sometimes our soul starts to speak to us and encourage us to heal.

I've included a great list of books for you in the resources section about the science behind fear. Much research and writing has been done on this topic, and rather than get you sidetracked with the formal scientific explanation here, I'd much rather you be able to dabble with the tools that will help you transform it.

For now, recognize that you'll need to feel in order to have fun with your fear. You'll need to feel stuff that feels like "survival" fear. You'll need to feel it in order to differentiate it from purpose-driven fear, the kind that'll move you toward your desires and dreams.

If you're able to recognize purpose-driven fear and have a kind of a conversation with it, you'll completely change the way you relate to the feeling and its resultant trigger inside you. This allows you to respond with the thought, belief, or action you desire, rather than the one your scared little girl keeps reacting with.

When I began training in John F. Barnes MyoFascial Release and Upledger CranioSacral Therapy, I was trained in not only how to feel but how to help others back into their body for the opportunity of healing. My teachers knew that to heal, we'd have to be inside of our body, and we'd have to practice feeling for authentic healing to take place.

Only that was always easier said than done. At first, nobody really wanted to be feeling their pain, whether it be mental, emotional, or physical. We were all terrified that if we started down that road of feeling, we'd be stuck in past trauma, not able to get back out again. That we might be re-traumatized. Many of my colleagues described such instances.

"She just left her body," I remember my instructor saying at a class one day. He was up on the stage and the client was lying on a massage table. I could hear her whimpers through the small black microphone John had clipped a quarter way down his blue button-down shirt.

"Okay, now she's back in, see?" John asked us to notice the subtle shift in energy and presence when his subject was feeling again. Many of us could see it, a recognizable way the body looked when someone was present and conscious. It was fluid. Warm.

We learned to recognize when a client was in or out of their body and how to help them back in. We learned to understand that guiding our clients to being in the body to feel was a real opportunity to facilitate their healing process, as well as a huge responsibility. Holding the space for someone to feel safe enough to feel is a skill.

This process, especially when someone has suffered severe trauma in their lives, is complex, and it requires a skilled therapist to facilitate a safe and effective healing process. For the best information on the SomatoEmotional process of trauma and healing from trauma, find John's book, *Healing Ancient Wounds*, and the book *Waking the Tiger* by Peter Levine, in the resources section for you.

"If you numb the pain, you also numb the joy."
—BRENÉ BROWN

After a trauma, injury, or illness, we often spend a lot of time, energy, and dollars on numbing our pain. As kids, we're taught to "brush it off," and are told, "you're okay," or "you'll be fine," even when we aren't or won't. We're taught not to feel. Our parents many times weren't equipped with the knowledge to help us feel or the understanding that feeling is a gateway to healing. Sometimes the people who tried to help us the most weren't capable of feeling themselves. They had no capacity or skill for it and so could not give us permission to feel. It put them too far out of their own comfort zone.

Later in life, we may suffer illness, injury, disease, and trauma and have to move very quickly back into the pace of life without fully healing from that trauma. The energy of trauma can then be stuck in the physical tissues of our body. Healing can occur at any time we decide to address what's stuck, leftover, or not fully resolved. Even something that occurred many years ago.

Have you ever heard someone experience healing later in life and say, "Whoa, I thought I'd already dealt with that!" I have. And it's an eye-opener. There are layers to the healing process. Feeling is the gateway to understanding your own layers and discovering how to go about peeling them away.

We know better now, so we can do better. We have the information and the science to help us understand that not only can we heal from our traumatic pasts and wounds, but we can overcome the residue of fear we live with as a result, begin to live with more joy, and even have fun with the feeling of fear for once in our lives.

Give yourself permission to feel everything without adding extra meaning. Start by pausing during your day to drop into your body and feeling senses to notice what you feel. Be curious. Don't be judgmental. Use a journal to help you process the sensations and thoughts.

There are a lot of things that get in the way at this point in the journey. The fear of feeling the fear is one of them. You might be worried you'll relive something, re-traumatize yourself, or open up Pandora's Box of feelings and not be able to get yourself back out.

Yet feeling is the path to the awareness you'll need to not only conquer the purpose-driven fear you're reading this book to deal with, but to have so much more fun with it too. Having a skilled therapist on your side might be key to moving through some of those more intense feelings. Someone who understands the somatic aspects of trauma will be very helpful. Check out the resources section for more on that. And you're going to want to interview your healers to find out how they go about the process of guiding you. I'm especially interested nowadays in practitioners who can hold a healing space for you and at the same time guide you to a shift, to a new way of thinking and believing about yourself and your trauma.

If you're reading this book, most likely you've already done a lot of healing work and you're interested in moving to another level, starting to share your story and message out loud, and moving through the kind of fear you're tired of: the purpose-driven kind. It's all a matter of feeling it and knowing the difference so you can take action on it before it takes you down or paralyzes you.

For now, let's practice.

What you'll need for the exercises: A notebook or piece of paper, a pen, and a timer.

Guidelines for the writing: Stay centered in your body. Connect to the breath. Move the words from the inside to the paper. Don't censor yourself. Write as fast as you can. Don't worry about spelling, punctuation, grammar, or finishing sentences. No rules, just write.

Exercise 6: Experience Feeling as a Gateway

Body awareness exercise. Find a comfortable place to sit or lie down. If you'd like to listen to a recorded version of this exercise, you'll find that here: https://soundcloud.com/lauraprobert/body-awareness-audio.

Close your eyes and start to connect with your breathing. Clear your mind and anchor into the senses. What do you feel? What sensations do you notice?

Relax your body, unclenching and releasing the weight of your body into the chair or bed. With every exhale, soften, release, relax, and let go a little more. Relax your head, neck, throat, and shoulders. Soften the space behind your eyes, through your jaw, and down through your throat and neck.

As thoughts come, release them and reconnect with the sensations of your body and breath. Relax and soften your chest, upper back, and torso, releasing all the way to your fingertips.

With every exhale, allow your body to get heavier and let go. Relax and soften your low back, belly, hips, buttocks, and thighs. Continue to clear your mind and notice the sensations of your body instead. What do you notice?

Relax and release your legs, knees, and feet. Feel your feet on the floor, the surface of your body on the chair, the clothes on your body, the temperature in the room . . . or whatever other sensation comes into your awareness.

Relax and breathe like this for several more minutes. Take a couple final deep breaths and slowly open your eyes. Move directly into the writing exercise without a break.

Write it: Set a timer for five minutes and fill in the blank: I feel
_____.

Speak it: After you're finished, try reading what you wrote out loud to yourself. Allow the vibration of your voice to inhabit the words and practice feeling once more. How does it feel to speak the words out loud? You might spend another minute or two writing about that.

If I was to highlight any part of this book, it would be this chapter and this exercise. I come back to it over and over in every class I teach and every moment I myself am stuck in fear.

If you've taken a class with me or read my last book, you'll surely recognize the prompt. That's because it takes practice to be good at feeling and noticing.

Recognizing fear as a feeling in your body takes away some of its power. Consciously practicing not adding any thoughts or meaning to that feeling reframes fear so that you can take action with the feeling, something I'll talk much more about in Part Three.

Feeling is the language of your intuition. Your intuition is the wise voice or inner healer that guides you in every aspect of your life. Feeling is the way you get the messages. Learning this language is important. We're born trusting it but quickly influenced out of that trust and skill.

Learning to feel and giving yourself permission to feel everything will be the way to the clarity you crave, the answers you seek, the next best step for your life, and the kind of purpose-driven fear-busting you will do. Feeling is how you'll know if the fear you feel is the kind you can use as a compass, or the kind you need to say "Hell No" to.

Let's get an even better feeling right now.

Exercise 7: Discover Pure Badass Clarity

Building on Exercise 2, the Hell Yes and the Hell No, we have to get good at feeling what it's like when we're undecided or confused.

"It's easier to be confused," my acupuncturist looked at me with her steel blue eyes and soft face, and I thought, *Oh my God, it is, isn't it?* Not making a decision was keeping me safer, inside my comfort zone. Rather than feeling the chest-cramping reality of my current situation, I'd rather just say I'm confused and let things play out.

But playing the waiting game was getting more and more painful and frustrating. The low-level resentment began to eat at my insides, infecting every single day with negativity, sadness, and hopelessness.

Let's do an exercise for clarity.

Body awareness exercise: Find a comfortable place to sit or lie down. If you'd like to listen to a recorded version of this exercise, you'll find that here: https://soundcloud.com/lauraprobert/body-awareness-audio.

Close your eyes and start to connect with your breathing. Clear your mind and anchor into the senses. What do you feel? What sensations do you notice?

Relax your body, unclenching and releasing the weight of your body into the chair or bed. With every exhale, soften, release, relax, and let go a little more. Relax your head, neck, throat, and shoulders. Soften the space behind your eyes, through your jaw, and down through your throat and neck.

As thoughts come, release them and reconnect with the sensations of your body and breath. Relax and soften your chest, upper back, and torso, releasing all the way to your fingertips.

With every exhale, allow your body to get heavier and let go. Relax and soften your low back, belly, hips, buttocks, and thighs. Continue to clear your mind and notice the sensations of your body instead. What do you notice?

Relax and release your legs, knees, and feet. Feel your feet on the floor, the surface of your body on the chair, the clothes on your body, the temperature in the room . . . or whatever other sensation comes into your awareness.

Relax and breathe like this for several more minutes. Take a couple final deep breaths and slowly open your eyes. Move directly into the writing exercise without a break.

Write it: Set a timer for five minutes and fill in the blank: When I'm confused, it feels like _____. Try to describe the actual physical and mental/emotional sensations, thoughts, and feelings that occur when you're confused.

You can go back to Exercise 2 now and add these important thoughts to those notes. You're building your cheat sheet. You're enhancing your awareness of when you're avoiding something that's a "no" inside you. You're giving yourself a way to address future feelings with better clarity and knowledge about what your own soul is telling you.

In the next chapter, I'll talk about how the energy of fear can reside in the fascia (connective tissue of your body) and how it is perpetuated by our thoughts and beliefs.

I'll introduce you to some of the top researchers of fear and feeling who will help you understand why you can trust the tools I offer later in the book. This will be vital for the moment when you feel like you're going to die, but your soul is calling you to take action.

And it will be the foundational awareness you need to create more fun with the feeling of fear and do the things you were born to do in the world.

CHAPTER 6

The Body and Mind
of Purpose-Driven Fear

I stared out the sliding glass door into the trees, rubbing the center of my chest with my right palm. The fear and anxiety was creating an ache there. *If you do this, you'll wreck everything*, I thought. A perfect example of me adding meaning to the fear feeling in my chest.

I was about to go find my husband and ask him for a divorce, for real this time. The fear was real. It felt like I was going to have a heart attack. I was nauseous. I was also so done that I knew there was no going back. This *was* going to go down. I let that part of me drive.

How do we know when to pay attention to the sensations of fear and take action to save our own selves and souls and do the bigger-picture healing we know we need to do? And how do we know when to retreat, when it's true survival fear, and we need to fight, fly, or freeze?

The confusion, uncertainty, and desperate attempt to talk yourself into something else when you know what you need to do is all part of the compass pointing you exactly where you need to go.

I found my husband that night.

"I want a divorce," I said.

And somehow the vibration of my voice moved with a tone different from the dozen past moments we'd both uttered the "D" word. There was nothing else clouding up the words. There was an—albeit terrified—clarity. It was about freeing my voice and saying the words even though I was afraid.

Even though my fear was in overdrive.

And here's the thing: when you're in physical pain, you can usually point to where it hurts. When you're afraid, you can also usually point to the place in your body the feeling is coming from. If fear is a physical sensation when stripped of the thoughts and meaning you've given it, then where is it coming from?

That's a question we can answer by paying attention to our bodies.

Purpose-driven fear has many of the same physical feelings as the kind of fear you'd end up in flight, fight, or freeze over. And it also has some characteristics you can learn to notice to be able to differentiate it from that survival kind of fear. The differentiation is the key. And that's a skill you can learn.

There are some questions you can ask yourself to help you know the difference. Grab your notebook!

Even though I'm afraid, would doing this align with a deeper desire?

Even though I'm afraid, would doing or saying this help me feel relieved?

Does this same fear keep coming up for me to address over and over again?

Is this something I've been wanting to say or do for a long time?

Does this action align with my deeper desires, dreams, goals, intuition, or vision for my life?

Am I afraid because I'm worried about what other people will think?

Am I afraid because I'm worried I'll make a mistake or fail?

When I think of saying or doing this is there an underlying excitement or feeling of purpose, mission or calling attached to the feeling?

Purpose-driven fear is just excitement without the breath. When we begin to recognize it in our body and move toward it with curiosity and inquiry, it shifts and becomes something we can use to help us point ourselves in the direction of where we want to go. It becomes a compass for our own success.

Was I having fun with my fear of asking for a divorce when that happened? That'd be a big no. There are some things in life that just aren't ever going to be "fun." Can I look back on that fear now, in retrospect, and see that the action was the "right" thing to do? Yes, I can. And that helps. Sometimes the relief, and even the fun, come after the action.

Major life decisions are going to be the biggest challenges to the idea of having fun with your fear. Major moments where you feel out of control, like the world is doing things to you rather than you choosing them, are going to be major challenges to this idea too.

Sometimes it requires taking a giant step back and observing our lives with a much, much bigger picture in mind. Why does everything have to feel so serious all the time? I think we were taught that it is. We are conditioned to add a negative meaning to the events of our lives.

And that's something I'm questioning every day lately. Can I have more fun even in the most serious, tragic, or sad moments of life? Good question.

Can we have more fun when trying new things that terrify us? I found out for myself that we absolutely can.

"Yes, I'd love to," I typed one day to my friend Miss Kiane. She'd sent me a message on Facebook asking if I'd like to be the featured poet at her Busboys and Poets event later that summer. I'm not really sure who typed "yes." Apparently, I was letting that bigger part of me drive that day, too. I was definitely having fun with the you-are-not-good-enough-to-do-this kind of fear that came rushing into my head as I read her generous invitation. I stopped. I took a breath. I chose a different thought: *there's no way in hell she'd ask you to do this if she didn't think you were good enough. Now just say yes!*

I said yes with that massive feeling of purpose-driven fear. And I was the featured poet at Busboys and Poets on August 20, 2019, with an adoring crowd of poetry lovers snapping and clapping me off the stage. Sometimes it feels good to feel afraid. I've since gone on to grace the stage with my words many more times.

THE BODY OF FEAR

I described a scene in my Myofascial Release class earlier where we were taught how to notice and assist a client who was out of their body. But why be in the body to feel at all? How does this help us heal?

Fascia is the secret to understanding the body of fear. When a trauma (mental, emotional, or physical) occurs, there's a transfer or shift of energy to you and in you. Depending on the circumstances of the event, that energy can enter into the physical tissues and especially the fascial (pronounced fash-al) tissues and get stuck.

Everything is energy and vibration. Fascia is affected by energy. It *is* energy. When energy is forced into your mind-body system, as in the case of any trauma, the fascia can be injured, dehydrated, inflamed, or otherwise damaged, and a restriction can ensue.

Over time, fascial tightness and restrictions can create abnormal and crushing pressures on vital internal structures and organs because of the body's natural tendency to compensate. Then you may begin to feel symptoms for problems that don't normally show up on X-rays or MRI's, leaving you frustrated and clueless on how to relieve the discomfort

In his article, *Traumatic Imprints*, in MASSAGE *Magazine*, John F. Barnes describes the process this way:

"The body then develops strategies or patterns to protect itself. These subconscious holding patterns eventually form specific muscular tone or tension patterns, and the fascial component then tightens into these habitual positions of strain as a compensation to support the misalignment that results. Therefore, the repeated postural and traumatic insults of a lifetime, combined with the tensions of emotional origin, result in tense, contracted, bunched and fatigued fibrous tissue."

THE MIND OF FEAR

John goes on to say that the cause of these kinds of problems is most often a combination of mental, emotional, and physical stresses and tells us that "researchers have shown that the type of stress involved can be entirely physical (e.g., repetitive postural strain such as that adopted by a dentist or hairdresser) or purely emotional (e.g., chronic repressed anger)."

Every single emotion you experience has a physiological effect in the body. Fear can sit in the physical tissues of your body in the form of the pent-up energy of a past stress, injury, or trauma.

We must begin to think of fear as a mind-body event. And we can address the feelings of fear by integrating our approach so that authentic (permanent and effective) healing can occur.

If you're suffering from past trauma, injury, surgery, mental/emotional/sexual abuse, or any other form of mind-body pain, you can explore integrated, alternative approaches to healing at www. MyofascialRelease.com.

Releasing the habitual physical and mental/emotional patterns of pain will be one of the ways you'll begin to move toward recognizing your purpose-driven fear. Knowing there are more layers to heal is the first step. Getting the help of a skilled practitioner is the next step.

In my own quest to understand authentic healing, I've been the joyful (and sometimes really pissed off) recipient of many different forms of healing, both psychological and physical. It's when the practitioner was able to combine those two kinds of modalities to treat the whole me that I experienced the most profound, intense, and lasting results.

I look forward to the day when our healers and healthcare practitioners are *all* trained in the psychology, physiology, and somato-emotional aspects of healing. With that integration will come true transformation, of pain and of our fear. I'm truly grateful to John Barnes and many of my other holistic practitioner teachers who persisted on their own journey through the critics and naysayers, trailblazing a path for us to follow. By doing that, they have created more leaders. And that ripple is real.

Be an advocate for your own authentic healing by searching for practitioners who understand the importance of integrating mind, body, and soul and who use techniques and tools that incorporate all of them in your treatment. Ask for recommendations. And then open your mind and be brave about trying new things. What if there's something you haven't learned yet that could change everything? I live by that question.

THE DIFFERENCES WITH PURPOSE-DRIVEN FEAR

In my attempt to understand the feeling of fear, have more fun with it, and to move through it and do the thing that scares me, I've begun to differentiate the survival kind of fear feeling from the purpose-driven kind. This book is about this purpose-driven kind of fear. We have to know what it feels like and how it's different than our primal, instinctual fears that protect us from physical harm.

Because the thing is, you're not going to die standing on a stage and sharing your message at the microphone. Well, I suppose something catastrophic could happen, but you get the idea.

You're also not going to die from speaking up to your boss or your spouse or your family about what matters to you. Or from writing your book, or starting your new business. Even though many times the fear makes those situations feel like life-or-death in your body.

This skill of discernment between the two kinds of fears is what allows you to use the feeling as a compass to point you in the direction of what you most want to do. And if you were paying attention earlier, you'll remember that it's this knowledge—in combination with a deep connection to the why of your desires—that helps you take action.

Aside from asking yourself the questions I listed above, there are some ways you'll learn to feel the subtle differences of purpose-driven fear in your body. And this is after you've shut down all the inner critic messages you're hearing that are giving that feeling extra meaning. We'll have a thorough chat about those inner critic messages in the next chapter.

What does purpose-driven fear feel like? Notice the areas in your body called the chakras. Chakras are energy centers and awesome places to tune into when you're beginning to understand all the connections and how they relate to fear. There are seven chakra or energy centers in the body, each with their own color association, emotional connections, and meanings. From top to bottom, they are:

The Crown (above the head)
The Third Eye (between the eyes)
The Throat (the front of the neck/throat)
The Heart (the center of your chest)
The Solar Plexus (just below the breast bone)
The Sacral (at the belly button)
The Root (at the tailbone)

Take a peek at the book *Chakras for Beginners* by Michael Williams if you'd like to explore the meanings and connections a bit further. The area of energy that the chakra encompasses is a three-dimensional, front-to-back, and side-to-side area of the body.

After spending some time noticing where the fear always showed up in my own body, I started to realize it was always around a particular chakra. And when I looked up the meanings and connections and colors and all the ways those energy centers integrated with the other things I was experiencing, I figured out that some of those sensations were old, habitual patterns that were not serving me anymore. The simple act of recognizing the pattern helped me understand the purpose-driven fear.

When you recognize an old, repeating pattern of feeling, get curious. What lies right inside of that information could be the key to releasing a pattern of fear you've been practicing your entire life. The awareness is the door to healing.

In my case, I'd often feel tightness around my throat or a choky feeling when I was faced with needing to speak up about something in my relationship. I also started to notice an ache in my low back, connected to my sacral and root chakras, and the feeling of not being safe. The low back I also later learned was a "kidney" area in the Eastern philosophy of medicine and acupuncture. And the emotion connected with the kidney is . . . you guessed it: fear.

Depending on the situation I was faced with, the feeling of fear would be more or less viscerally intense: heart pounding, legs weakening, or nausea. I'd have to resort to my list of questions above when I noticed I was not in a life-threatening situation. I had to check in with my current reality and remind myself I was safe. I used these tools to gain awareness and eventually to master the awareness to the point where I now know when I should act with the feeling.

And standing at the open mic about to recite a poem did not count as life-threatening. Even though my heart was attempting to tell me it was. And so was the full-body sweat and shaking.

I learned to take the hand of that terrified little girl, look down at her, and say, "We've got this. We can do this together." I learned to make some space between me and the feeling of fear, recognize it as outside of my true self, and then take some action. It's that awareness that helped me do what I was afraid to do. It was aligning with my desires that helped me know the actions were bringing up purpose-driven fear.

I'm still afraid when I speak to groups of people, small or large. The difference now is I use that feeling as fuel. I remember my purpose, my why, and that it's not really about me anymore. My fear of not-good-enough is boring. What if something I share changes someone else's life? I can be more brave when I hold these ideas in my mind as I walk up onto the stage. In Chapter 8, I'll be giving you some more tools to differentiate purpose-driven fear from other kinds of fear. For now, let's move on to those inner voices that might be holding you back.

CHAPTER 7

The Inner Critic Voices

In Chapter 4, we called out and wrote down a list of the inner critic voices. They're the messages constantly moving through our minds telling us something unhelpful, unhealthy, or just plain untrue. They had a purpose once upon a time, but they aren't serving that same purpose in this current stage of life. We don't need to hate on them. We need to recognize them for what they are: a waste of time. It's time to ditch those suckers. But we can try to be nice about it.

When I learned to not only recognize my inner critic but make friends with her, things changed. When I decided to take control over the messages and replace them with more helpful, healthy, aligned, positive, and on-purpose messages, I began to manifest my dreams.

I'm not typing that last line lightly. My life began to change in ways I only dreamed about, as soon as I realized that my power had been sitting there in my ability to choose my thoughts and beliefs. And your power is sitting waiting for you to claim it as well. As I read more and more about positive thoughts and manifesting the things we want in our lives, I'm realizing that it's more important to decrease the negative, toxic thoughts than it is to grasp for the desires. The former almost instantly up-levels your energy vibration. And that's a good thing.

In a later chapter, I offer some positive affirmations to use to replace the negative beliefs, but for now, know the awareness is the first step. The awareness is the foundation we're building this playground on. And we want a magnificent, solid, sturdy foundation.

The thing about your thoughts and beliefs, and the messages that play like old recordings in your mind, is that they were taught to you. You were taught "the truth" once upon a time, and you used that truth throughout your life. The past truth may not be the truth now. It's a moving target. And many of the truths you were taught don't serve you at all anymore.

You are now older, wiser, and more badass. You recognize the old beliefs that don't serve you anymore. You're beginning to question them. That's good! And we called them out and wrote them down so when they show up again, we'll have a better chance to recognize them quickly.

Let's take this to the next level. Let's have a full-on conversation with our inner critic. The inner critic isn't something you can hope will go away. This part of you wants to protect you. Once upon a time, it had a purpose. There was a time in your life when you needed it, and it was doing a good job of protecting you. It helped you survive. In some cases, it may have saved your life. It's not a part of you to reject. It's a part of you to wholly accept and befriend.

Now that you've done some healing work, are enhancing your awareness and beginning to change your life goals, the voices also must change. But they're not, are they? They're the same old, conditioned, unhelpful voices coming up again and again to "help" you. Retraining your mind and those messages is the path to moving through the fear and having fun with it.

You're not good enough, I hear. You don't have anything they want to hear. Nobody's going to want to read this, the nasty voice continues. Sound familiar? Damn that voice. Seriously, I'm sick of it. Sick of the noise in my own badass head trying to sabotage the good I've come to this world to deliver. I'm tired of being my own reason for not shining. I'm ready to master this practice of befriending and detaching from these voices so I can get on with expressing the words that'll heal myself and the world.

This is an especially difficult challenge for those of us who've decided to embark on the entrepreneurial journey and be responsible and accountable for our own living and happiness. We automatically take on the task of dealing with the inner critic, whether we knew that was part of the job description or not. For some of us, that means constant anxiety. And an important part of self-care is going to be managing that anxiety, which means not just managing the voices and messages we're getting but doing something more helpful in those moments to propel us forward.

For the people who had no idea their inner voice could be so cruel, unrelenting, and paralyzing, I hear you. But it's going to be so worth the healing work you'll need to do when you get to a point of hearing those shameful and damaging messages and can say something like, "Hey, I hear you. Thanks for the concern, but I got this," and quickly spin around and walk in a better, more purposeful direction, headed straight for what you desire for your life.

This action—hearing the voice, recognizing it as destructive, and then talking to it with authority over who you are and what you want—is the key to befriending, detaching from, and mastering your inner critic. The awareness comes first.

Esther Hicks reminds us, "Desire's the seed of all creation. It's why we're here, to want what we want and create a life we feel good in. Our 'rockets of desire' shoot out into the Universe and the Universe hears the call. It's our one job to selfishly thrive; to follow, align and vibrate with things that feel good." The message in our head tells us the opposite. And we learned to listen to those messages like they are God, or the Pope, or whatever other authority figure you deemed worthy of your worship.

We've been taught wanting is greedy, that we should focus on the needs of others first; that that will create a worthy, worthwhile, honest life. We've been taught we're bad if we want more. And that we'll go to Hell if we don't do what's right. Can you tell I was raised by a few religious people?

We've been taught wrong, and the inner critic messages we listen to and believe are worth exploring. Noticing and understanding them will change everything. This isn't for the purposes of bashing them or any of the people who taught us. They were just doing the best they could with the information they had at the time. The purpose is the awareness and the choice you get when you have it. You get to choose something better, more healthy, more joyful, more peaceful, more grounding, more calm, and more aligned with your essence, which is love.

Somewhere along the line, I learned that wanting more was greedy. That helping others should come before me, that wanting more meant I wasn't grateful for what I have, that my desires aren't as important as the needs of others, and I was a bad mom, wife, or employee if I prioritized my desires over caring for my kids, or spouse, or boss, or whomever.

After following those rules for a couple decades, I was left "having everything" but feeling exhausted, unhappy, and resentful. It didn't make sense. I did what my momma (and teachers, coaches, friends) told me, and I felt like I was in prison. But it wasn't just you, Mom. It was all the influences around me that I gave priority over my own intuition and inner guide. It was what I was making all of that mean in my head. And now that I know more about it, I can make changes that greatly affect my ability to thrive in my life. I get to take back responsibility for all of it. That's exciting. And maybe, Mom, you'll realize that all of this was the most perfect journey I was meant to take to get to where I am today: helping lots of people feel and live their best, most awesome life.

THE SECRET TO FINDING MY DREAM LIFE

After learning about awareness and about my inner critic, I realized the rules I followed were someone else's. I learned they didn't all apply to me, and they weren't the end-all when it came to joy. I learned I could create my own joy, peace, calm, gratitude, love, and whatever I wanted on a daily basis.

I had to unlearn what I was taught and go on an adventure of discovering the truth—my truth—even when I was judged harshly for it. Even when everyone else said something different. Even when someone didn't like the way I was doing things and told me so. Even when that person was my father, teacher, boss, coach, best friend, or spouse.

Understanding my inner critic messages would be the key to unlocking my prison cell. The courage to pursue my dreams and desires would be the secret to feeling I'd finally arrived in a life I was meant to live.

Here are five inner critic messages specifically relating to desire that you need to notice, analyze, and ditch to help you realize that wanting more is what you were born for and the path to living a fulfilling, joyful, healthy, and purposeful life. They're not the only five. And we'll get to some detailed tools later in the book for dealing with more of these kinds of messages. But for now, see how these resonate and play out in your life.

1. **Wanting more is greedy.** Actually, wanting is natural, and it's how dreams come true. Not wanting things is abnormal. You're a co-creator of your life. Wanting is how you create. Don't let anyone make you think differently. Time to let go of this ancient, sabotaging belief and choose something that serves your joy.

Notice this inner critic voice from outside yourself by using awareness to take a step back and analyze it. How do you know this is true? Who taught you? Recognize that your thoughts and beliefs come from what you were told or taught by people who were told and taught by their people. What makes it true or right?

> *"Whether you think you can*
> *or you think you can't, you're right."*
> —HENRY FORD

The power is in the awareness. Time to think differently.

2. **Helping others should come first.** Actually, if you don't prioritize yourself first, you'll burn out and feel exhausted, sick, and resentful. And then you'll be no good to anyone. People-pleasers and care-takers seem to be born into this role. But it comes from seeking approval and not feeling our worth as a birthright. This awareness will be life-changing. Stand up inside your worthiness and recognize you have one person to take care of first: you.

When you're happy, healthy, and fulfilled, your cup is overflowing. You'll be able to serve well from this overflow, never limiting the energy and abundance coming to you. When you're tired, a little sick or resentful, you'll be serving from reserves at best and there's a limit to your ability to serve without seriously compromising your health, wellness, and joy.

Fill your own cup first. Get it to overflow. Then feel how wonderful sharing and giving your time, energy, and resources starts to feel.

3. **Wanting more means I'm not grateful.** Actually, both can happen. Feeling grateful's the path to feeling good. So gratitude comes first. But your desires are okay too. And changing your mind is natural. In fact, you can expect your desires to change and expand as you go. Being grateful for what you have helps you feel good

now. Wanting something more or new will help you align and fine-tune with joy on an ongoing basis. It's possible to be grateful and reach for more.

> *"The reason you want every single thing you want*
> *is because you think you'll feel really good when you get there.*
> *But if you don't feel really good on your way to there,*
> *you can't get there.*
> *You have to be satisfied with what is*
> *while you're reaching for more."*
> —ABRAHAM HICKS

4. **What I desire doesn't matter, compared to other people's needs.** This's a version of "wanting more is greedy," and actually, your desires matter because you were born. In fact, it's your desires and the pursuit of them that changes and heals the world. Ignoring your own desires will turn you into a zombie. And when you follow your heart and soul's desire, you align with that joy, you become a magnet for more, and, with that abundance, you can give generously to those who've had bigger challenges than you.

> *"Don't ask what the world needs.*
> *Ask what makes you come alive, and go do it.*
> *Because what the world needs is people who have come alive."*
> —HOWARD THURMAN

Following, aligning with, and pursuing your desires does not mean you don't help people along the way. It just means you realize the pursuit of your dreams and desires is the way you help others. In other words, you'll help most when you're pursuing your own desires!

5. **Going after my desires is irresponsible** (makes me a bad mother/ friend/wife, etc.). What about my kids? You wonder. Well, the best and most important thing you can do for the people you care about the most is take care of your own health and happiness. Because like the "other people's needs matter more" bit, if you ignore your own for too long, you'll be a hot, sick, resentful mess. Ick.

What you're teaching your kids by pursuing your desires and dreams is that theirs matter too. You're teaching them to live a healthy, happy, purposeful life. You can't teach them this important thing if you're teaching them everyone else comes before your own desires. You teach by example, by the way you're living every day.

What's truly responsible, brave, and world-changing is the ability to go for what makes you happy and healthy while taking care of business—the kids, the dishes, etc. You can do both. Your happiness and health do not have to be your sacrifice. You might just think they do. If you sacrifice your own health and happiness, you risk dying with serious regrets.

"Oh my God, what if you wake up some day, and you're 65 or 75,
and you never got your memoir or novel written;
or you didn't go swimming in warm pools and oceans all those
years because your thighs were jiggly and you had
a nice big comfortable tummy;
and you were just so strung out on perfectionism and
people-pleasing that you forgot to have a big, juicy creative life,
of imagination and radical silliness and
staring off into space like when you were a kid?
It's going to break your heart.
Don't let this happen."

—ANNE LAMOTT

Don't let this happen. Don't allow someone else's rules to keep you stuck. What feels good? Your desires are sacred breadcrumbs that'll lead you to joy. You were born to follow that trail!

Laura Munson offered a badass exercise and tool in her Haven Writing Retreat that I've kept with me for years now. I'm going to couple it with the body awareness exercise because it's this embodied awareness that will be the door to the creative and intuitive connection that gives you the clarity you crave. Let's practice.

Exercise 8: Name Your Inner Critic Voice

Body awareness exercise: This one is slightly different than past chapters. Find a comfortable place to sit or lie down. Close your eyes and start to connect with your breathing. Clear your mind and anchor into the senses. What do you feel? What sensations do you notice?

Relax your body, unclenching and releasing the weight of your body into the chair or bed. With every exhale, soften, release, relax, and let go a little more. This time, I want you to think about your inner critic voices, and especially the one that feels the worst or triggers you the most.

This might be one of the versions of "not good enough" you encounter when you're doing something new, exciting, or a little scary.

From that list of voices you made earlier, which one comes up over and over again? Which one gets you stuck the most? Breathe into your body as you allow the feeling of that to surface so you can notice it.

If you were going to assign a name to this voice, what would that name be? Open your eyes and write it down.

Write it: Write down the first name that comes to you.

When your voices have a name, you get to separate from them. It's an awareness that will serve you in the future. If the voice pipes up and you recognize it, you can have a conversation with it.

This has been done before, I heard. *Who are you to think you can do this any better or that anyone will want to read this?* The voice continued.

"Thanks, Martha, but I got this!" I said and continued typing away on my book that you have in your hands now. I learned that recognizing and naming that voice in me that was only piping up to protect me from shame and humiliation was how I was going to retrain my mind to choose a better thought.

When I named my inner critic, she no longer lived inside my head. Naming her put her somewhere outside of me where I could deal with her. The awareness gave me a choice: continue to believe and be paralyzed by that voice, or have a better conversation with Martha that I could respond to. Awareness is the key to every single self-sabotaging thought or belief you have.

Having negative thoughts is one thing. Believing those thoughts is quite another. Believing them and making them mean something else begins to paralyze you. And then believing them to the point where you stop taking action on your dreams is just nonsense. You'll have to be consistent with this practice. And it will pay off.

Purpose-driven fear bubbles up to protect you. There's something inside you that's invested in your happiness, in preventing you from being shamed or humiliated. It wants to keep you safe in your comfort zone to minimize risk of mistakes and failures. It likes it when you're content, but if it had a choice, it'd keep you in that "meh" state forever, where you're not overly happy, overly sad, or really feeling emotions of any extreme.

Have you felt the "meh" I'm talking about? It's no fun anymore, is it? You're a world-changer. You're ready for the adventure and ready to take the risks. "Meh" is actually starting to feel painful, suffocating, and intolerable.

To be that kind of warrior you're going to have to play bigger with your fear and master the mindset that got you to this place of "meh." To have fun with fear, you'll need to be able to take risks that make you feel vulnerable, tolerate those feelings, and then realize you're bigger than them and take some action to move through them.

Martha is much quieter now. I think she gets that I've figured her out. She still tries, but not as loudly. And because I'm great at that conversation, she feels safe enough to give up a little quicker and let me get on with my badassery. When I figured out how to make friends with her and not resent every time she showed up, the game started to change. And the vibes raised a level higher.

Having fun with fear is mostly being able to listen to your mind and laugh a little. Realize how silly those paralyzing thoughts are, and then pick better ones. The ability to do this over and over again will require you to practice feeling into and taking a power pose inside of your worth.

The ability to then take bold action for your dreams despite the feeling of fear and the risk of failure will require the agility, grace, and strength of detaching from the outcome of those actions and dwelling inside the powerful knowing that everything that happens, happens *for* you and not *against* you. Everything.

Developing a strong trust in the Universe helps. Knowing you *are* the Universe will up-level your badassery. When you reframe bad events as redirects and look for the lessons and possibilities, you'll quickly realize you can stop judging the stuff of your life. Everything is an opportunity. Everything.

Here's an exercise that will help you stand on a strong foundation of awareness when you're coming up against your purpose-driven fear.

Exercise 9: Claim Your Worth

You were born, so you're worthy. What will it take for you to believe and embody this statement? It was a process for me, filled with not one magic moment but several linked together that built upon each other and gained momentum. The closer I moved toward my joy, the faster the worth refilled and fueled my soul.

Worth is funny. We learn so early on that there are conditions to it. When in reality, the simple fact that we're alive gives us full access to our worthiness.

> *"Self-worth comes from one thing—*
> *thinking that you are*
> *worthy."*
> —WAYNE DYER.

In fact, I have a coach friend who disagrees with Dr. Dyer. He says you don't even need to think it, because you're already automatically worthy, whether you think you are or not.

And that's why I have this piece in the "Inner Critic" section. The only problem with our self-esteem and worth is that we don't think highly of ourselves. We've relied on others to give that feeling of worthiness to us. Which is how we give all our power away. And when the messages from others were, "You're a bad girl," or "That's inappropriate," or, later in life, "Don't brag!" or, "Don't be unprofessional," we learned that our worth was based on what we were told by others, based on our actions.

If the others in our lives were not great at helping us feel good about ourselves, or worse, taught us the opposite, we carried those beliefs into adulthood and continued to feel we were unworthy, unlovable, inappropriate, unprofessional, etc.

Let's practice claiming our worth.

Body awareness exercise: Find a comfortable place to sit or lie down.

If you'd like to listen to a recorded version of this exercise, you'll find that here: https://lauradifranco.com/brave-book-resources/.

Close your eyes and start to connect with your breathing. Clear your mind and anchor into the senses. What do you feel? What sensations do you notice?

Relax your body, unclenching and releasing the weight of your body into the chair or bed. With every exhale, soften, release, relax, and let go a little more. Relax your head, neck, throat, and shoulders. Soften the space behind your eyes, through your jaw, and down through your throat and neck.

As thoughts come, release them and reconnect with the sensations of your body and breath. Relax and soften your chest, upper back, and torso, releasing all the way to your fingertips.

With every exhale, allow your body to get heavier and let go. Relax and soften your low back, belly, hips, buttocks, and thighs. Continue to clear your mind and notice the sensations of your body instead. What do you notice?

Relax and release your legs, knees, and feet. Feel your feet on the floor, the surface of your body on the chair, the clothes on your body, the temperature in the room . . . or whatever other sensation comes into your awareness.

Relax and breathe like this for several more minutes. Take a couple final deep breaths and slowly open your eyes. Move directly into the writing exercise without a break.

Write it: Set a timer for five minutes and fill in the blank: My story matters because _____.

Speak it: Take a moment to read your written words out loud to yourself. Let the vibration of your voice move through the words. How does that feel? You might write a little more about it afterward.

REALIZING YOUR WORTH

I suppose there was one day when my worth came back and hit me like a Mack truck. That's a good thing, in case you're wondering. I needed to be smacked by it. I noticed that when I was doing things I loved, I felt very worthy. It was like joy had this way of making me feel not only alive, but the purpose and magic of life coursed through my veins while I was lit on fire with joy.

There were moments along the way that filled me with joy and built up my self-worth. Remember the story I told you about teaching my first class at The Writer's Center? The feeling is hard to describe. I could take you back to the moment of my children's births. Reaching down between my legs to feel my daughter's head moving out of me and into the world. Whoa. Yes, I'm worthy.

Crossing the finish line of my first marathon and realizing I'd done something not many people would ever be able to do gave me a feeling of peak elation that made me feel worthy. And yet I realized at some point that accomplishments—even giving birth—didn't define my worth. I could list many right now. I was really awesome at being a perfect good girl. I was awesome at accomplishing and achieving things. I was a master list checker-offer.

But what I do isn't who I am. What I achieve is not who I am. And if I'm not anything I do or achieve, then what exactly makes me worthy? Who exactly am I?

"I'm always wondering these big things about life," I said to my boyfriend this past year. We were sitting in the car together, and my mind was racing, again.

"My mind is constantly filled with wanting to know the bigger answers, to understand my purpose," I continued. "And I feel exhausted some days in that, trying too hard to feel into an answer I may never really get."

"Yeah, none of that stuff is really on my mind very much," he replied.

"I take things moment to moment, and I'm not pulled into the trap of worrying much about if I'm living my purpose or not."

When I'm having conversations with people who matter to me that both allow me to be myself and give me perspective about how other people think and do life, I smile with knowing. What do I know? I'm just feeling joyful in knowing that it's the differences that give richness to our lives.

Speaking out loud to my boyfriend, a safe place to be these past few years, has helped me to be afraid and say it anyway. The pattern of men in my life was one of attack or negativity in the past. The new pattern I've created is one of acceptance, awareness, and healthy, conscious conversation. It's been an incredible relief to know people like this. And it's been an incredible blessing to have one to love.

Let's do an exercise to get in touch with the inner wise badass who wants to start speaking up more in the world.

Exercise 10: Explore Being Unafraid

Body awareness exercise: Find a comfortable place to sit or lie down. If you'd like to listen to a recorded version of this exercise, you'll find that here: https://lauradifranco.com/brave-book-resources/.

Close your eyes and start to connect with your breathing. Clear your mind and anchor into the senses. What do you feel? What sensations do you notice?

Relax your body, unclenching and releasing the weight of your body into the chair or bed. With every exhale, soften, release, relax, and let go a little more. Relax your head, neck, throat, and shoulders. Soften the space behind your eyes, through your jaw, and down through your throat and neck.

As thoughts come, release them and reconnect with the sensations of your body and breath. Relax and soften your chest, upper back, and torso, releasing all the way to your fingertips.

With every exhale, allow your body to get heavier and let go. Relax and soften your low back, belly, hips, buttocks, and thighs. Continue to clear your mind and notice the sensations of your body instead. What do you notice?

Relax and release your legs, knees, and feet. Feel your feet on the floor, the surface of your body on the chair, the clothes on your body, the temperature in the room . . . or whatever other sensation comes into your awareness.

Relax and breathe like this for several more minutes. Take a couple final deep breaths and slowly open your eyes. Move directly into the writing exercise without a break.

Write it: Set a timer for five minutes and fill in the blank: If I wasn't afraid, I would _____.

Speak it: After you're finished, try reading your written words out loud to yourself. Allow the vibration of your voice to inhabit the words, and practice feeling once more. How does it feel to speak the words out loud? You might spend another minute or two writing about that.

Life is what you think it is. If you think something is scary or that making a mistake or failing will make you unworthy, then it will. If you feel into your purpose-driven fear, say, "Thanks, Martha (fill in with your voice's name), but I got this," and carry on with taking the action that your future self would thank you for, you're on the right track.

The feeling of fear means whatever you make it mean. Why not start to make it mean something different? Check yourself when the old thoughts come up. Create new truths for yourself. You can write some of them down if they are coming to you right now.

Now we'll get into some of those badass tools that are the actions you'll take to get you through the fear, laughing with it and starting to look it in the face and say, "Bring it on!"

Your fear does have a sense of humor. You've never given it a chance to come out and play like this before. It's going to tease and taunt you. It's going to challenge you in every possible way. You'll see her tongue sticking out at you sometimes. When you invite her into the sandbox with you, be ready to play. This will be a whole new world, and possibly the best one you've lived in yet!

The biggest magic trick to changing your fear to fuel for your dreams is the action. People have interesting ideas about what that should be. Part Three of this book is going to offer you tools to use for each of the boring, unhelpful inner critic messages and fears that come up when you're playing bigger and louder in the world. But let's end part two by helping you master feeling the difference between paralyzing purpose-driven fear and necessary survival kinds of fear. Time to take it to the next level!

Remember to join me in the free Facebook group, Brave Badass Healers, a Community for World Changers for extra support and conversation around these topics.

CHAPTER 8

Practicing the Difference between Purpose-Driven Fear and Survival Fear

When I started really studying the difference between the visceral sensations of "real" survival kinds of fear and the purpose-driven kind I'm sharing about in this book, I realized that most of the time the physical sensations were so similar, it was no wonder I couldn't overcome them.

The body has a natural, primal protection mechanism that we're born with to keep us safe from harm and threat. Fight, flight, or freeze helps us not die. But since nobody is being chased by a saber-toothed tiger these days, we have to understand when those reactions are happening unnecessarily. We need to know how to differentiate the reactions from those happening due to purpose-driven fear—the kind we really would benefit from overcoming.

And I began to notice a pattern of attributes of the purpose-driven kind of fear, a way to understand if it was fear I could face and use as a compass or fear that was giving me a warning to stay away. Other than the absence of a tiger, there are great questions to ask and ways to know if you can use the feeling to your advantage and act with it.

First of all, purpose-driven fear is more excitement than anxiety. We notice the difference in the feeling, because behind the fear is an excited

93

feeling that has a message that goes something like, *whoa, what if I could really make this happen . . . how cool would that be?* Even though the feeling itself might have a competing message like, *I think I'm going to die.* So dramatic, that voice, right?

Ask yourself, "Does this feeling keep surfacing? Does it keep coming up asking me to deal with it?" The purpose-driven fear is a part of you that knows your desires, dreams, and goals. It's a force that's *for* you; it's your cheerleader and coach. It wants you to do this, so that situation and feeling are going to rise up in you repeatedly. It's your soul's way of saying, *hey, don't ignore me; this matters!* It's the voice of your inner guide and knowing.

This one might sound obvious, but there's purpose behind purpose-driven fear. The thing that's making you feel like you're going to die if you do it is actually on the list of your goals when you look at and review those. It's something that aligns with your mission, purpose, and calling in the world. When you're feeling the fear, you might ask yourself, "Is this on my list of goals?" And then go review those goals to see.

Purpose-driven fear usually has a meaning attached to the feeling that you'll find on that inner critic voices list. It's very clearly attached to a self-sabotaging thought or belief. And it's more complicated than "I feel like I'm going to die." Go check that list again and see. When you find the voice attached to the feeling, you can begin to have that conversation with it and let her know, "I got this!"

Purpose-driven fear is very often about a consequence that has to do with someone else's rule or opinion. Similar to the inner critic messages list, realize that when the fear is about what someone else will think or do, you've given your power away. Center back into your fiery purpose and ask yourself, "What matters to me the most?" Ground yourself in the fire and inspiration of your purpose. Remind yourself why you're doing this. Realize that what others think is none of your business, and carry on.

Lastly, you might just ask yourself this simple question when faced with the feeling of purpose-driven fear: Does this matter to me? If it's a yes, then it's something you can practice taking action with.

Exercise 11: Discover How Purpose-Driven Fear Feels

Body awareness exercise: Find a comfortable place to sit or lie down. If you'd like to listen to a recorded version of this exercise, you'll find that here: https://lauradifranco.com/brave-book-resources/.

Close your eyes and start to connect with your breathing. Clear your mind and anchor into the senses. What do you feel? What sensations do you notice?

Relax your body, unclenching and releasing the weight of your body into the chair or bed. With every exhale, soften, release, relax, and let go a little more. Relax your head, neck, throat, and shoulders. Soften the space behind your eyes, through your jaw, and down through your throat and neck.

As thoughts come, release them and reconnect with the sensations of your body and breath. Relax and soften your chest, upper back, and torso, releasing all the way to your fingertips.

With every exhale, allow your body to get heavier and let go. Relax and soften your low back, belly, hips, buttocks, and thighs. Continue to clear your mind and notice the sensations of your body instead. What do you notice?

Relax and release your legs, knees, and feet. Feel your feet on the floor, the surface of your body on the chair, the clothes on your body, the temperature in the room . . . or whatever other sensation comes into your awareness.

Relax and breathe like this for several more minutes. Take a couple final deep breaths and slowly open your eyes. Move directly into the writing exercise without a break.

Write it: Set a timer for five minutes and fill in the blank without censoring yourself. Purpose-driven fear feels like _____.

Speak it: Read your written words out loud. The vibration of your voice will shift the energy and amp up the awareness.

Throughout your practice, remember to journal your notes, thoughts, aha's, ideas, and lists about all of this. You'll be able to go back to those things as a reference when you need a reminder or you're having a particularly trigger-y day.

Now let's get into Part Three: tools to deal with more of the inner critic messages and thoughts that come up to paralyze you. I'll cover the common ones that are usually getting in the way of you being you and sharing your unique gifts with the world. Get ready to bust them up and have a little more fun. We're going to learn how to feel and take action at the same time.

Fear as a Compass

Feeling and differentiating fears and actually taking action with the feeling are two different things. Each of the seven chapters in this section explores specific kinds of inner critic messages and fears in order to reframe them, desensitize them, and begin to have way more fun with them.

When you start to realize all the extra meaning you're giving to your fear, you'll be able to take the action required to transform that fear. Using the feeling of fear as a compass is the next level of fun and where the magic begins. But it's the awareness that's the key for all of it. The more awareness you have, the more you'll begin to feel like a master when it comes to having more fun with your fear.

The Magic is the Action

Go ahead and light your candle
you can even smudge your space
pray to your guides
and gods
and angels
to help you through your day.

Write out all your wishes
your dreams, your goals
and desires.
Say your mantras
on top of them
and chant up to the skies.

Wave your feather
in the air
pay homage
to your spirit creatures
shove your crystals down your bra
set your alarm for 333.

Listen to your intuition
notice what she says
make a big-ass plan
to change the world
and even
tell your friends.

But please hear this
my Goddess friend
if you don't take action
if you just keep wishing
on a star
and hoping it'll happen

You'll be sitting there
with your crystals
and your candles
and your sage
and nothing much will happen
nothing much will change.

It's time to do
what you're afraid to do
to feel it and be brave
to make the call
to write the words
to ask for what you want.

Cuz if you think the magic
will work
without this step
I'm afraid you'll be disappointed
and stuck
and pissed as heck.

It's time to walk your walk
do the things you preach

to sing your song
and dance your dance
even if you gotta
make believe.

It's the action
that's the magic
it's the action
that'll create your dreams
It's even the mistakes and failures
that'll manifest these things.

So here's a challenge for you
if you're up for the task
do something a little scary
something big or small
breathe courage every day
live brave and free your soul.

CHAPTER 9

Your Fear is Boring

Your fear of not-good-enough is boring. It's not about you anymore. What if the thing you're still a little afraid to share is exactly what someone else needs to hear to change or even save their life. It's time to be brave.

Those are the three sentences I put together and now consistently repeat to myself after realizing that my story, shared out loud, would possibly save someone else's life. When I read Elizabeth Gilbert's Facebook post about my fear being boring, something clicked, shifted, and opened up in me. I combined that with Anne Lamott's quote about telling our stories, and it was like I had this badass word arsenal that resonated so deeply in me, my marrow was shaking.

I began to know with my whole soul that sharing my stories was what needed to happen if I wanted to help others. I began to feel in my heart that if I did it from an aware, compassionate, kind, authentic place, nobody would get hurt. They might be triggered, but they wouldn't be hurt. And what's to say that triggering someone isn't the best possible thing you could do for them? What if that moment of trigger opens up a whole, incredible, new, and wonderful world to them they never thought about before the trigger?

In the healing world, they call this a healing crisis. This is when you feel like everything is about to come crashing down, but in reality, everything is just reorganizing to handle the healing shift happening inside you and prepare you for a new chapter. Would you be willing to feel the "pain" if you knew more joy sat on the other side of it? "Depends," you might be saying. "How much pain are we talking about here?"

Only as much as you can handle, is my answer. Because you control this game. You control your reactions and responses. That's actually the only thing you have control over in this little thing we call life. But many times, it's enough. When you're responding to the stuff of your life with awareness, everything can change. It's a matter of if you're going to let all the excuses get in your way one more time, or if you're willing to move toward that purpose-driven fear, feel something, and then take some action with it.

I happened to be paying attention when my Facebook messenger pinged on May 16, 2017, at 3:39 p.m.

"Greetings from NYC. I've followed your page for a few months now. I just wanted to know if you have any links or articles on finding 'the relationship' with yourself. Translation in a nutshell: I'm a mom of five (ages 3–18). So depressed that I do not know who I am. I don't know that I'll ever figure it out. I'm almost to the point where I don't want to be anything, not a mom, not a counselor, not a best friend . . . I don't have time to be myself to my own self. Thank you for listening to my ranting. Any materials would be much appreciated."

I was happy to get the message and amused that I'd seen it that day, as it was on my business messenger, a place I don't frequent.

"Hi Shirley," I replied to her while I opened up another screen on my computer to get to some articles. "I hear you. I see you. Yes . . . give me until tomorrow, and I'll have something for you. Sending big love."

I sent her a message the following day, as promised. "Let's start with this . . . give me a message back anytime."

"Thank you!" Shirley replied. "I've read this twice so far. Going to read it again in the morning before the little one wakes up. Definitely taking notes and I can't wait to start scheduling some time for myself. Time to find out more about me."

I decided to go one step further for my new friend. I wrote Shirley a blog post and dedicated it to her anonymously. I asked my audience of moms and healers to step up in the comments if they had advice, support, or love for her. And they did. It was amazing.

Shirley and I kept up our communication and began to develop a friendship. She signed up for a course I was running, became a part of my brave healer community, and started to make some very positive changes in her life. She then went on to write her own two blogs. One of them was a story about her journey with depression and the other a call out to other mothers to let them know they weren't alone.

I later found out that Shirley had been suicidal and planning the note she'd write to her husband and five kids. I swear if this one thing—those few words on a blog and the effort I made to support a total stranger at a time when she needed some hope—is the only thing I ever do in my life, it will have been enough.

It's not about you anymore. Your fear of not-good-enough is boring. I'm here to blast all of your excuses. There will be a few that seem like really good ones, but I want you to go ninja on them and really take a deep look at why they paralyze you still. Is the purpose-driven fear too much for you to handle? I doubt it. Be a warrior. Be a trailblazer. Jump through the wall of fire. Step into the arena and get your ass kicked. It will be okay.

And you just might find other warriors in there with you. You might realize that there's a community waiting for you if you're willing to show the world who you are and what you're about. You just might understand for the first time in your life what your true purpose in this world is. And you may just recognize that the years of fear that preceded this moment were training you to be in this very moment. It was all good. And now it's time to do something different.

What I love now is calling myself out on the boring bullshit my inner critic tries to pass off as real or real dangerous. I've lived after speaking on stage enough times now to know I'm not going to die sharing my story with others at a microphone with bright lights on my face, even if I have to shake like a leaf while I do it.

What's a new way to think about what's happening, and what are some tools you can use to turn it around? Next we'll tackle the fear of what others will think if you do what you want to do.

CHAPTER 10

What Everyone Else Thinks is None of Your Business

"You own everything that happened to you. Write your stories. If they wanted you to write warmly about them they should've behaved better."

—ANNE LAMOTT

God, I love that quote. When I first started writing for the world to read, I had to put this up on my computer, and I had to remember to read it out loud every time I'd hit the publish button.

It's not that I was in for upsetting people, and I certainly did not have the intention of hurting anyone. I wanted to heal me. I wanted to help others. And to have a mission like that meant I'd have to be a trailblazer. And that meant I had to share some things that weren't all sunshine and roses, some truths that showed the uglier side of people and relationships.

As a healer, I found myself asking my clients to do the vulnerable work of healing but realized I'd have to go first. For me, going first means writing the thing that everyone else is thinking but is too afraid to say out loud. Feeling afraid of upsetting, offending, or disappointing someone is a strong trigger for fear. We base our survival on the love and connection with other people. It's a real need. In caveman days, being part of your tribe was how you survived. Being cast out or rejected meant certain death.

So when we consciously do something that could possibly trigger someone and cause an unwanted reaction toward us, it's scary. We'll avoid it at all costs. We react from a primal fear of rejection. Unless that something has to do with our soul and its ability to feel free.

Writing about my family, friends, acquaintances, colleagues, and others who know me is easy when I'm saying something good about them. It's harder when the feeling is not so good and the old adage "if you can't say anything nice, don't say anything at all," is in my head.

What if there was a way to express, through writing or speaking, ideas that explained your current feeling state from a personal perspective, without putting anyone into attack mode or on the defensive, or otherwise upsetting, offending, or hurting them?

That was what I was after. I needed to write to feng shui my soul. I needed to use the writing to give witness to my truth. Some of that writing was for my eyes only, the feng shui required to create a space for the inspired messages to come through—the ones the world would read.

In the beginning, it's good to drop expectations of what the writing or the speaking is. It's best to not censor it. Moving it out of you is the healing process. The healing process needs to happen so that your enhanced awareness can grow. It's with that enhanced awareness that you'll be able to move real words from your heart to your tongue or pen and write for the world.

Those are words that will change the world. What are you still afraid to write or speak?

I remember back as I was beginning to submit my words and ideas to bigger online blog sites, and I chose to write about being triggered by a comment someone made in a Facebook group and how that trigger affected me. *Elephant Journal* took that article, chose a new title and photo for it, and published it for me. That article was the first that went "viral" for me, receiving hundreds of thousands of views and thousands of shares.

The whole experience was exciting and somewhat terrifying. Nowadays, I tell my brave healers this: it's not about *if* you'll be criticized, it's about when. It will happen. And if you expect it, maybe your trigger won't be as harsh as the one I felt hit me in the gut the day I started to read the comments on my article.

Out of hundreds of positive comments, I chose to focus my attention on the one that was negative. Out of hundreds of beautiful, "me too," head-nodding feedback, I got sucked in and let the one toxic comment hit me so hard, I reeled for a week. I stopped writing that week. I was paralyzed by the feeling of "bad girl."

What had I done? Written something someone disagreed with. Yep. And rather than reading that comment with awareness, I read it and took it personally. I had somehow written something wrong, bad, stupid . . . whatever. Holy smokes, I can feel the trigger mildly resurface as I recall the story for you now. Damn those triggers, right?

I'm going to repeat the title of this chapter for you now. What everyone else thinks about you and your opinions is none of your business. Don't take anything anyone says personally, especially if that someone does not hang out in the inner circle of people that really matter to you.

I believe that last paragraph is worth writing on a sticky note and pasting to wherever you need the reminder the most. I wish I'd had it up the week this all went down. Thing is, when I look back at this moment—at what happened, how I felt, and what ensued afterwards—I see it all as a fantastic healing opportunity. I'm not going to say I have extra special armor now that protects me from feeling badly when someone disagrees with me or doesn't like me or what I say. What I will say now is that when that happens, I surely don't spend a week dwelling there. I'm a badass at feeling the feeling, not making it mean anything, and then moving on to something that serves my mission and purpose in the world. I think of Shirley and carry the fuck on.

Thing is, when you're brave enough to start moving your ideas out into the big, bad world, the big, bad world will begin to respond. And the people in the world are of all kinds, many of which will not like you. And that's totally okay. Your job in the world is not to have everyone like you. In fact, if everyone likes you, you're not doing this right. If everyone likes you, you're trying too hard to fit in. And my guess is that's becoming rather exhausting.

In fact, many of the ideas that get the most attention from the masses are ideas that divide people. So if you're willing to stand up for what really matters to you and write or speak something that is polarizing, my guess is you might have a viral blog too.

What was the line that irked my reader that day? It was about following your heart instead of your mind. He did not accept that as a great way to be in the world. He completely disagreed with me, and I sulked off that day (week) into a little cave of shame because, I thought, *maybe I got this all wrong.*

Opinions aren't wrong; they're just opinions. You get yours. I get mine. And if we don't agree to disagree when we need to, then fires start. I've come to believe that the best way to be in the world is curious. The best way to really understand each other is to step into the other person's shoes and get curious about the life they had to live to get to the moment and opinion they are so ruthlessly defending. Awareness and compassion are essential here.

Someone have an opinion that's different than yours, an opinion you know without a doubt is right? Get curious first. Ask yourself some questions. Why do you believe what you believe? What were you taught?

How can someone else believe something different? Is it possible both people are "right?"

There's some hint of world peace in the idea of staying curious rather than defensive or, worse, offensive. But people get hot and bothered about their opinions, don't they? They go on the offensive. Their spewing feels like an attack sometimes, doesn't it? I call toxic on those moments and choose to walk away. You'll know when there's no mutual attempt to be curious and understand each other. You'll know when it's appropriate to walk away. Listen to your intuition on this one. And if your habit is to stay and fight, especially with someone you know will never come to the middle, rethink your tactics. Be more curious. Back away when it starts to feel tight, constricting, or suffocating.

I have so much more fun with my fear of being wrong or bad these days because of this one realization: everyone is walking around with their opinion of life based on a very unique lens they're looking through. How can one lens in seven billion be the "right" one?

There will be many times you disagree with someone based on deep-seeded beliefs. What I like to do is reflect on my own thoughts and beliefs enough to see where I'm still being too rigid, or where my upbringing created something that no longer serves me. I wonder a lot about how new thoughts and beliefs would serve my current dreams, desires, and goals. I'm willing to be wrong with someone if it means I get to learn a new way of being that brings me more love and joy.

And that's the key, to monitor the feelings and understand how they fit into your plan for more love and joy. If we keep it simple like that, the fear of what everyone else thinks will dissolve, and we'll be more apt to enjoy hearing what other people think just for the sake of understanding, learning, and evolving and not taking it as a personal attack against us or who we are in the world.

Exercise 12: Identify Who You Would Become

Body awareness exercise: Find a comfortable place to sit or lie down. If you'd like to listen to a recorded version of this exercise, you'll find that here: https://lauradifranco.com/brave-book-resources/.

Close your eyes and start to connect with your breathing. Clear your mind and anchor into the senses. What do you feel? What sensations do you notice?

Relax your body, unclenching and releasing the weight of your body into the chair or bed. With every exhale, soften, release, relax, and let go a little more. Relax your head, neck, throat, and shoulders. Soften the space behind your eyes, through your jaw, and down through your throat and neck.

As thoughts come, release them and reconnect with the sensations of your body and breath. Relax and soften your chest, upper back, and torso, releasing all the way to your fingertips.

With every exhale, allow your body to get heavier and let go. Relax and soften your low back, belly, hips, buttocks, and thighs. Continue to clear your mind and notice the sensations of your body instead. What do you notice?

Relax and release your legs, knees, and feet. Feel your feet on the floor, the surface of your body on the chair, the clothes on your body, the temperature in the room . . . or whatever other sensation comes into your awareness.

Relax and breathe like this for several more minutes. Take a couple final deep breaths and slowly open your eyes. Move directly into the writing exercise without a break.

Write it: Set a timer for five minutes and answer the following question without censoring yourself: If there were nobody left to offend, upset, or disappoint who would I become? You can also use the words "what would I say" or "what would I do?" Remember, don't get stuck on the words of the prompt themselves . . . just move what's coming through to the page. If the timer goes off and you have a lot more to write, then write. Move it all out. This is one of those prompts that tends to uncover some interesting old, unhelpful thoughts. You answered it in Exercise 3. This time, go a layer deeper.

Speak it: Now take a moment to read your written words out loud to yourself. Putting the vibration of your voice to your words is important. And if you want to write for a few more minutes about how that feels, that's great.

This last exercise is powerful, and there are layers to it. Come back to it when you find yourself stuck about what someone else thinks of you or what you're doing in the world. Ask yourself some questions about that person:

Does this person matter to me?

Why does this person's opinion matter so much?

What outcome do I fear if this person thinks negatively about me or what I'm doing?

Am I willing to risk losing this person over this?

Is expressing myself going to help me heal?

What's more important to me: risking offending this person or healing myself?

When we're caught up in the fear of what others think, there are usually some toxic thoughts going on. Comparison can be one of those. Do you find yourself wanting what they have? And are you allowing their opinion to weigh on you heavily because of that?

All of these questions serve to enhance your awareness and give you the tools to change your perspective and retrain those inner critic thoughts . . . or our reactions to criticism from outside ourselves.

For example, I keep my website blog open for comments because I love getting nice, joyful messages telling me how awesome readers like you think my writing is (and how awesome I am by extension) and how my words inspire you. And also because differing ideas and suggestions about my blog topic can enrich it for the next reader. But once in a while, a troll shows up. It's our greatest fear, right? That's why I approve all comments before they're published on my website blog. Except we can't protect ourselves everywhere. My bigger site blogs all have open comments. And I accept that I will be dealing with some people who don't agree with what I have to say.

This is why some folks don't open their blogs to comments at all. I'm sure they feel much safer knowing they can freely express without fear of negative feedback or criticism. I dabbled with that idea once upon a time. The "Approval First" route won out, though, even though it's a little more work; the positive comments and insights make the extra effort worthwhile.

I think being open to all comments is a stage of evolution where you just don't give a fuck what others think, to the point of not taking any judgements personally and/or not feeling triggered when it happens. Wouldn't that be nice? It's the process of healing we've been talking about here. You can get to that stage.

I know some of you are there already and are sitting pretty in that feeling of no-fucks-left-to-give. What about those of us who still get triggered when we receive judgments that are negative, or even mean, feeling the pang of shame rise from our gut to our face? How do we evolve into the being we crave, who's able to read or listen to negative—or even mean—feedback and understand it's never, ever personal? The being who understands that it's actually so many other things rather than personal? I'm interested in this way of thinking myself and getting way better at it.

At this point, very few comments trigger me, but if I'm honest, I'll admit that once in a while, when someone has an opposite opinion which makes me feel wrong or stupid, the pang in my gut in combination with the flush in my face will remind me that shame still lurks in the crevices of my heart and isn't fully detoxed yet. The shame trigger is real and a little bit evil.

There are some people who are better at creating that trigger than others. Can you think about when it happens to you? Who's the person that triggers it the most in you? For many years, that was my dad. "I don't just love you for nothing," he said to my sister and me, no doubt just trying desperately to get us to behave on a weekend when he was exhausted by having to take care of us. Still, that line is forever tattooed in my memory.

My ex-husband is another one. "Your parenting is questionable," he said one day when we were discussing our kids and my part in raising them. And that was a good day. My mom and best friend are on my trigger radar as well. They matter to me. I've given their opinions a certain weight in my life. And that's the important piece to this. If the person matters, then how are you going to listen, stay aware, and respond instead of react? If the person does not matter, then why are you sitting there still playing the game, wasting your time, and giving up all your energy?

WITH AWARENESS, WE HAVE A CHOICE TO THINK, BELIEVE, AND ACT IN A BETTER, HEALTHIER WAY.

And that's the tool I want to talk about now, as it relates to no longer giving a fuck about what others think or say, and having more fun moving through the fear when you're worried about other's opinions. It's a practice that's helped me desensitize myself to negative feedback so that it's not always triggering the shame as such an intense visceral hit to my body.

I believe this awareness is badass, meaning you'll need to develop it and create a discipline or practice of it. It takes perseverance and a bit of determination, as well as courage and an ability to feel and tolerate feeling vulnerable, but knowing how to move yourself to a state of peace, calm, and relaxation quickly.

I practice tools that have helped me do this, and we've been learning them in this book. Here are a few in a nutshell:

1. Know the details of what triggers you (who, what, how, when, where). When you start understanding the trigger in all its gory details and can recognize the inner critic thoughts that go along with the chest tightness or sick-to-your-stomach feeling, you are a step ahead and on your way to the awareness that will make a difference for future rounds. So instead of running in the other direction, get curious and detached. Ask more questions. Get to know the feelings and sensations. Recognize the habitual way you go about reacting to the triggers. Watch yourself like you're watching a movie.

2. Practice awareness of the feelings and thoughts associated with the trigger. Notice your habits. This piece of knowing the trigger is important. What are the physical sensations? Describe them. Where are they in your body, and what do they feel like? What are the actual thoughts you have? And what are you making those messages mean? Curiosity and inquiry is key here, as is massive self-compassion.

3. Write everything out. Journal everything in detail, until you have nothing left to write about it. This is so that you can up-level the awareness. When it's out of you, you clear some space for something better to take its place. So move the ideas, thoughts, reflections, and aha's to the page, where you can read, look at, be curious about, and assess them.

4. Call out the shame as fast as possible by speaking it out loud to someone. This works faster than almost anything I've done and is sometimes the hardest to do. Calling out the shame can feel embarrassing.

However, if you can call it out, out loud, to someone you love and trust, you'll find the shame dissolves almost as immediately as the words leave your lips.

5. Flip your switch to something that serves you better as fast as you can, and focus there. Here's where you choose something else that's better, healthier, and more aligned with who you are and want to be, to think, believe, and do. Your awareness will be the key here. You notice how you feel and what you think, you write it down or call it out, and then you choose a better thought or action to practice. You shift the energy to something that feels good. I use gratitude and love lists for this purpose, as well as actions that my future self would thank me for. Basically, I remember my purpose and aim there.

I find myself practicing these steps in different order, depending on the circumstances. They all have to do with awareness. So I call a friend when I need to. I take out my journal when I need to. I notice my body and my thoughts (a daily practice). And I've become a master at knowing when, why, and how something triggers me. I've decided to be brave about calling it out, out loud, when it happens, with people I trust, so it doesn't live rotting inside me.

One last tip that's the bomb when it comes to not caring what others think: **Surround yourself with people who love you**, who you *do* care about, and whose opinions you trust, value, and respect. Stick with the ones who uplift you on a regular basis, and unapologetically leave the rest.

Now, let's deal with that sneaky little question of TMI (Too Much Information). Versions include, "Is this too much information?" And, "Am I being too real here, or sharing too much?" The TMI fear is funny to me. I'll help you find the humor in it too.

CHAPTER 11

Is There Any Such Thing as TMI?

Can a person be too raw and real about their life out loud? Does being vulnerable create perceived weakness? Can the vulnerable one be a leader? All great questions you'll need to answer for yourself, but I am about to call bullshit on them anyway. Here's why. Even if all of these things are true for you, I'll find someone else who says the opposite. That's the thing about life: everyone has a different opinion. Who gets to be the authority? Who's right?

My thoughts on the subject are the more personal your story, the more universal your message. Can you dig it?

What if the very pain you're afraid to share is exactly the thing that will save someone's life?

I offered that idea in a recent workshop. Let's get moving through your fear and sharing that thing you're called to share. There's no TMI. And there are eleven ways to move through the fear that your sharing is too much, too vulnerable, or too personal for your readers, family, co-workers or anyone else in your life.

"That's what happens when you share about your divorce on Facebook," a friend recently scolded me. I laughed at him and said, "Yeah, I guess so. Oh well." This was immediately after I confided in him that an old (very old) boyfriend had just "found" me there.

Was I surprised I was found out? No. Curious? Totally. The online world is big and brutal. If you want to play big these days in terms of your message, you're going to have to open your heart, practice fierce boundaries, and allow the energy to bounce off of your armor. Armor that you then must take down before you share your next message.

There are a small percentage of us who can be vulnerable enough to share our authentic healing stories with the world and then carry on like it's nothing. Only it's not nothing. It's totally a big something. We're the ones being called right now to share. We're the ones who will redefine TMI. We are warriors.

"This book saved my life." A friend and mentor of mine said those words one night at an open mic, when I failed to promote my own book to the crowd. She went on to talk about the book and said, "And she laid out her business there for us to read," with a look in her eye of *I'm not sure I would have done that, but thank you for doing it.* I took the complement it was meant to be and had to suffer a visceral moment (just a few seconds' worth) of "inappropriate" in my gut.

Our ability to be real, raw, and a little too much is how we heal ourselves and the world. TMI? I can't think of any. The stories I shared in my book? My truth. And that's all they need to be to help someone else.

If it happened to you, chances are it's happened to someone else. If you've thought of it, believed it, experienced it, and/or survived it, chances are someone needs to hear your story so they can move through their own wound without feeling so alone. This is what #metoo is all about.

The judgment of TMI is about the receiver being unable to handle/process/hold a loving, healing, non-judgmental space for the sharer. It's also about old, outdated, unhelpful rules you were taught that you're following now, even though they don't serve you anymore.

I'm out to wake people up to this realization, because awareness, authenticity, and courage are what we all need right now. If something is TMI for you, then push it aside for now. Explore how you feel about it first, before you fire off your judgment. Question your ability to tolerate another human being's truth, whatever that truth may be.

This came up for me a few years ago after writing a book that talked about my childhood wounds.

"You better not publish that!" A family member said to me after reading parts of that book . . .

> *"You own everything that happened to you. Tell your stories.*
> *If they wanted you to write warmly about them,*
> *they should've behaved better."*
>
> —ANNE LAMOTT

That quote's so good, I had to type it again for you. I've used this quote so many times recently—to many a head nod, I might add—that I've memorized it. But here's where I get caught up now. Just maybe, at the time of their "bad behavior," they were just a stupid, unconscious kid. So what's a healer to do when compassion has taken over and she's learned how to forgive? Do I still share? Yes. Because it's what's going to heal us and the world.

And here are eleven ways to help you move through the fear:

1. Stop thinking and start feeling.
2. Write or speak from this feeling place.
3. Write or speak from your own perspective.
4. Write or speak without blaming.
5. Write or speak the facts from a place of forgiveness.
6. Write or speak with the intention of healing.
7. Write or speak with the energy of gratitude and love.
8. Write or speak with the goal of helping.
9. Show us, don't tell us.

10. Write first without the expectation of publishing.

11. Get feedback (if you must).

Here's a brief breakdown of each and how it will help. Mostly, this is about your awareness, your intuition, and your mission in the world as a healer right now. This is about learning to write, speak, and share your stories in a way that feels good, authentic, and brave, but that will also move people. Sharing a "sort of" personal story that others can tell you're holding back on? I'm not sure it's going to get you the response you really want. Time to be brave.

1. When you realize you're over-analyzing, over-thinking, and adding baggage to your already heavy baggage, you need to stop. Clear your mind, drop into your body, and start feeling. Try connecting with the breath, your body, and your intuition, which will give different messages than your mind. Practice reconnecting to that place often.

2. The writing we're aching to share comes from the heart and soul, not the brain. As soon as you're following old rules about what's right, appropriate, and professional, you'll lose the feeling behind the words, and the writing will sound cold, robotic, and boring. Write from an energetic, feeling state. You have to practice getting into this state before you write and practice staying in it during the writing.

3. When you write from your experience, perspective, and opinion, what's too much? It's yours. Go back and read that Anne Lamott quote again. If you're saying you're too much, you're telling us that too. When you own your stories and share the facts of them, you're being authentic, and we can trust you. You give us permission to be that too.

4. Take responsibility in your writing for everything in your life. As soon as you start blaming others, the story takes on a different

energy and will be misconstrued. Talk about how you felt, instead. Talk about what happened inside of you when the event took place. If you follow the words of the book *Radical Forgiveness* by Colin Tipping, you'll understand that everything is spiritual perfection, and you don't need to blame anyone for anything.

5. Carrying on with the forgiveness topic, when you write from a place of forgiveness, you're giving yourself (and the reader) that gift. You've heard it a million times: forgiving is not for the wrong-doer, it's for you, so that you can live free. Write from that place, and what you share will give others permission and courage to forgive as well.

6. When you share a story, you're healing yourself and your reader at the same time. So as you begin to write, ask yourself: What would be the most healing thing I could share here? Then write from that intention and energy.

7. Energy is everything when it comes to *everything*! So, when you write your story, the energy you're feeling while you're writing matters. Not feeling inspired today? Or worse, feel downright pissy? Then hold off. When you're writing or speaking that story you've been afraid to write, or worried you might be sharing too much of yourself, your energy will be the thing that helps you get over your fear and be authentic and brave. Practice vibing higher.

8. Similar to the energy conversation, what's your intention with the writing? You want to help others, right? Explore this a little. When you sit down to write, you can ask yourself the question: How can I best help others by sharing this story? What angle should I take on this piece that'll be the most helpful? Then connect to your body and intuition and write from that feeling space.

9. When you tell us, instead of show us, you're going to sound bossy, stiff, and unemotional. Show us instead. Use scenes and dialogue

to help guide us into your story. Give us perspective, suggestion, and feeling. When you show us, we will feel it, and when we feel it, we begin to heal.

10. This is my favorite go-to for when I'm scared. I pull out my journal and write just to feng shui my soul. I write every possible detail, just the way I want to write it, and then I can go back and decide if it's the story I want to share, or if there's another version ready to flow out of me. In other words, just sit down and write. Don't censor yourself. If the thing you write isn't for sharing, that's okay. It might be the clearing you need to do so that the story you'll share moves through you. Just write.

11. Read your piece out loud to someone you trust and get some feedback. The most helpful feedback I get is in my writing group online. I post things I'm afraid to share otherwise and ask for feedback. I have a safe space where I can share my most vulnerable things, and I trust those ladies to be real with me. This kind of community is priceless. One note of caution about feedback. Don't allow the feedback to overrule your intuition about anything. Use it to validate your feelings. If it doesn't resonate, learn how to say, "Thanks," and move on. Find my free writing group, The Write Habit: a Brave Healer Community, on Facebook.

We're all human. There's no TMI. If you're a professional following confidentiality rules with your clients, I'm encouraging you to share stories you feel good about, not stories that compromise what you do as a professional. There's a way to do this.

The most important thing about sharing our stories is the idea that everyone is on the same playing field as a human being in this world, all living our lives, exploring what it means to be alive and in connection with others, and seeking understanding about what brings us health and happiness. We're all one. We're all equal. Telling someone that their share is TMI is rejection of their soul, the human being existing in the world with you, taking the same adventure you're taking. Pause before you judge.

When you think about life and your role in it, if you're inspired to share, there's a reason. Follow that ache. Be brave, and let's heal together. Let's start a movement. How about instead of TMI we use MIP (More Information Please!)?

Next we'll tackle fear of failure and completely reframe it so that you realize you're in charge of never failing again.

CHAPTER 12

What if I Fail?

During the writing of this book, I experienced a couple events that I'd usually call failures. And what do I do when I'm triggered by what feels like failure and the associated feelings of not-good-enough? Write. I've learned to use tools to shift my energy from triggered and paralyzed to neutral or, even better, to joy. Here's a poem I wrote during one of those weeks.

How's Next Tuesday?

There was a knock at the door
and I knew
so I peeked through the hole first.
I shouldn't have opened the door
but I did.
Failure and her sister Mistake
wanted to have lunch.
"Sorry, I'm busy writing poetry," I said.

They persisted.
I resisted.
They convinced.

I winced.
They went on and on.
I recognized that boring song
and I closed the door in their face.

Another knock came.
And muffled words from outside the door,
"We're not what you think we are,"
they pleaded.
But the fear of what others would think
if they saw me having lunch with the enemy
sunk in and I said,
"Go away, I don't want to play today."

The following week my phone rang.
A familiar number showed
so I pressed green.
"Hello?"
Failure was back on the line and this time
it was clear: she had an agenda.
Fear flushed through my gut
to my cheeks
but before I could hang up
she eeeked out the words,

"I swear I'm your friend."
I was curious.
"What do you mean?"
"You always seem to make me feel bad,"
I said.
"You always make me feel stupid and sad."

She sighed.
"That's you feeling that way," she replied.
"That's you thinking I'm something to avoid.
That's you making your heartache mean more than it should."

I was confused.
"What do you mean?" I asked again.
"Every time you visit
I'm reminded I'm not enough.
I'm sure others will see you and steer clear.
Nobody wants to be seen with failure!" I shouted,
sure I offended her, but not caring.
Failure was amused.
"What if you needed me," she said.
"What if you'd never succeed without me?" She teased.

Now I was mad.
"What the fuck do you mean by that?"
"Relax, take a breath," she said.
"If you never get to know me,
if you never learn to dance with me like that,
if you never take risks and fall,
or start the journey toward your dreams,
by seeing me repeatedly,
you'll never understand,
you'll never succeed.
Because it's failure you need
to get anywhere worth going."

I stared at the phone.
Took another deep breath.

And realized.
I'd been hiding all my life
from the one thing
sure to get me to the place
I've always longed to be.
And the more she showed her face,
the more I hid,
not realizing I should have been
excited instead.
Because one more date with failure
meant one more step toward my dream.

"So how's next Tuesday?" I said.

Embrace the fact that failures are stepping stones and stop calling them failures, and you'll very quickly be having way more fun with your fear of failure. You must fail. You must fail a lot. You need these experiences to know what you're made of, learn, grow, get better the next time, and really get clarity about what it is you love. And . . . every failure gives you a story to share.

If you're afraid of failing, you may have a feeling inside you that failure means something else. Not good enough ring true? Unlovable? Stupid? You'll recognize some of those inner critic voices when you're triggered by fear of failure.

The voices can be nasty, but we're past that already because you've been cultivating the awareness about all this to the point that you're calling out those voices on the regular. Don't stop now with failure. Don't make these moments mean anything. Realize that you gave something a shot. You made an effort. You learned something about yourself. Be proud that you were willing to take a risk and learn the next best step. Failure is absolutely necessary to live a great life.

Over the past year, I've had so many failures, but two stand out to me. I have a new acquaintance in the poetry world who invited me to her open mic night here in Maryland. It was a different kind of poetry thing: a poetry slam. I hadn't been to a slam before. I'd heard some, but honestly I really didn't understand the difference between a slam and a regular poetry night.

So I showed up with a poem to read. Turns out, you needed three poems. A slam is where you bring three poems, one in each of the categories listed, and get scored for your performance of them. At the end of the night, after all contestants have read their three poems, you get a score from the judges.

When I realized I didn't have three, I decided to scramble and search my phone for a couple more. They really weren't "slam" poems. Actually, the one I brought wasn't either. But I didn't know any better.

I was one of five contestants. I came in fifth. One of the best slammers in the country (the *country*, y'all) was there competing that night. I had a moment where I felt like a complete idiot failure. But it was all good. I learned a lot that night. I learned that I should prepare more. I learned what a slam was. I learned about that kind of poetry (which totally turns me on and which I must learn how to write). I learned that I can lose—like, really lose—and win at the same time. I learned that I won't die after failing miserably in public.

The learning continued a few days later as that terrible feeling of "loser" sat in my chest and gut. I posted on Facebook about it. That was therapeutic, because many of the people who were there commented to help me feel better. But that doesn't totally make you feel better, does it? I had to come back to my own worthiness again. I had to stop making my failure mean I was anything but a warrior.

Will I try something new like that again? Yes, for sure. Will I try to prepare myself better the next time? For sure. Do I love poetry so much I'm willing to suck at it to get better? Hell yes. And that's why we need to have more fun with the fear of failure. It's the potential for greatness that sits in the moment of learning. The potential for superpowers. If you can look the fear of failure in the eye and do that shit anyway . . . believe me, you have a superpower most don't.

I'm remembering another moment when I saw something come across my inbox. It was a TEDx practice day in Wilmington, Delaware, just a short drive from where I live. I'd thought a lot about giving a TEDx talk, been coached by someone who'd done one, and made friends with another. I knew I could take advantage of the practice day and possibly get the attention of the Wilmington director. In fact, I'd met him a few weeks before at a publicity conference I was attending. I was there to learn how to pitch major media. I signed up to speak to him, knowing that a TEDx talk was on my list of goals for my business. I was nervous, but I thought, *what the hell, it can't hurt to meet the man.*

He liked my idea. At least, he said he did. And when I mentioned I'd be at his practice event a couple weeks later, his eyes lit up. He was excited to know that I'd heard about it. I shook his hand after my two-and-a-half minutes were up and said, "I'll see you in Delaware."

By the day of the event, I'd written and gone over my talk, but I hadn't memorized it. Life got in the way in the weeks before the event, and I didn't have time to memorize it. Actually, if I'm being honest, memorizing it terrified me. I now know that I sabotaged myself. But I digress. On the day of the event, I brought my notecards. I was the only one that day who used notes.

I went in knowing I'd be the only one using them and decided that was what "practice" was for. I gave my talk. It was fine. But, of course, I didn't wow anyone. The video that was promised as a part of my fee was not usable. I should've complained, but unfortunately, they can't go back and shoot it again, so it was what it was.

The whole thing felt like a big disappointment and failure. But I learned a ton. The biggest thing I learned from doing the event was that doing a TEDx talk was no longer something on my bucket list of things I feel I really want to do. This was huge. There are many reasons I came to that feeling, and not being able to do it was not one of them. In other words, I know I could do it. I just don't want to anymore.

Clarity is sweet. It helps you redirect. And that "failure" helped me redirect in a big way. I know now that I want to speak to audiences, but I want to gift them with poetry. I also want to gift them with my imperfect, sometimes not memorized, sometimes completely unrehearsed but fully intuitive self. The perfection of a TEDx talk no longer helped me feel excited about sharing my message. And right there I knew, from the feeling of it, that I'd be happy to let go.

And I want to compare this to the feeling I had after the poetry slam. This was a warrior's kind of feeling of "I'll do better next time," and "I totally want to master this!" And "I can't wait to learn how to do this in a way that turns people on."

[Side note: Since the time of this writing and meeting Shirley, I have decided I will continue to pursue the TEDx goal. Stay tuned.]

Feel the difference? It's the feel that matters here. It's the feel that has me having more fun with the fear. It's the potential for fueling my own fire, for helping warm others with that fire, and for the possibility of some bigger thing or feeling. It's the question that comes up: What else is possible here? I love that question. And I love being inspired to ask it!

Now I'd like you to think about some of the past moments of your life you once considered a failure. Which of those moments do you now recognize as stepping stones, learning tools, or opportunities to improve, grow, or evolve?

Which moments created within you a bad feeling of wanting to hide? Which created that feeling but then quickly morphed into, "What else is possible here?" Move forward by moving through the feeling of the fear of failure with a new way to look at it. What can I learn today? Who can I meet today? What's something I can take away from this? How will this make me better?

Then let the seeking for those answers be your focus, instead of the feeling of doing something bad or wrong. Stay in curiosity. Stay in your beginner's mind. And watch how everything changes in your future pursuits. If you're wanting to experience a life worth living while feeling fiercely alive and enjoying your wildest dreams coming true, you must fail, and you must fail many times.

Next we'll tackle that voice that wants to let you know, "It's already been done . . . who are you to do this any better?" And here's a hint: It may have been done before, but not by you! Imposter syndrome sucks. And it's total bullshit.

CHAPTER 13

It's Already Been Done

It for sure has already been done, said, written, or created before, but—listen closely—not by you!

The voice that tells you something like, *this has been done before; who are you to try to do it better,* is one of those nasty messages that will stop you up quicker than anything. Don't listen to it. If ignoring that message is just not that easy for you and you're starting to believe it's true, what I want you to know is that there really is very rarely an original idea that exists.

Did you all read that piece in *Big Magic* where LG talks about this? She was telling us the story of a book idea that she waited too long to act on and that she eventually saw another author friend had started writing about. What's a girl to do when she realizes her idea is now no longer her own?

Well, you'll have to pick up *Big Magic* for the rest of that story. It's a great book. For now, I want you to understand something about creative inspiration and the Universe. If you're inspired to do something, and the Universe has bestowed this amazing idea upon you, please take advantage of it and go create. Do not let the message that it's been done before keep you from doing it *your* way.

After teaching my workshop, *Writing as a Path to Healing,* several times both online and locally at The Writer's Center, I had a curious email arrive in my inbox one day that said, "You can buy *Write to Heal* now on Amazon!"

What the fuck? I thought in my head. Who was this person, and how did she steal my information? I was sick to my stomach. I hadn't written that book yet. I of course *had* written a couple other books with my version of writing to heal in them. But that title. That was mine.

Turns out, you can't actually copyright a book title. So I took a deep breath and decided to delete the email, not explore any further, and carry on with my writing to heal in the ways only I could. Because even if one hundred people are doing what you're doing, they are not you. I promise you, they're not doing it like you're doing it.

There have been several times I've seen "my" work online now. The internet is a big, bad place, and people do steal stuff. But more often, people are just getting the same divine inspiration from the Universe. We are all picking up on what the world needs right now. There are several of us doing the same kind of work. And that's okay.

Guess what? We need all of us. We need all of us because there are seven billion people on the planet and no one person can serve all of them. We need a hundred hot yoga teachers. We need a million meditation teachers. We need as many artists as we can get. And we need as many people to write their stories as possible. More authors? Yes, bring them on! Ten stories on the same topic? We need them all.

This is not a competition game. This is one big divine collaboration, and if we'd just realize our unique part in it and ignore the messages in our heads that we're making up about how we're not good enough, we'd be in action toward saving the world instead of paralyzing ourselves into doubt.

Yes, it definitely has already been done before. Honestly, probably several times. I don't really care. I want to see your version. Because your unique voice might be the only voice I can hear or resonate with. Your specific story, in just the way it happened to you and in just the way you tell it, might be the reason I can learn from you, respect you, or be able to really hear you.

Your version is the one that matters to someone. Your expression of it is the version that someone needs. Your ability to communicate it in the exact way you do is why someone's light bulb goes off. And isn't that an amazing thing?

Go. Do. Your. Thing.

Another version of this fear goes something like, *who am I to…?* This Impostor Syndrome is something I have to call bullshit on. The thing is, no matter what your story is, no matter how much experience you have, no matter how many degrees you've received, classes you've taken, or years of practice you've completed, you're going to be a step ahead of someone who needs your help.

We all have to start somewhere. I remember being a new physical therapist working with a mentor in a huge hospital in their orthopedic department. I felt so inexperienced and inept. I was learning from the best, most experienced mentors. I was learning hands-on techniques I hadn't learned in school. Every day that went by, I learned new things, practiced and mastered techniques, and helped people. Even though I'd just graduated from school.

When you're not feeling good enough, you must stop and celebrate what you *do* know, what you *have* done and who you *have* helped. You must keep your mind focused on gratitude for the knowledge, experience, and awareness you have. When you're staying open to that kind of magic, the knowledge, experience, and awareness you need to keep you moving forward is easily recognized.

As the mom of an aware, gorgeous, fearless, and intelligent teen, I'm often mowed over by the wisdom of the things she says. Does what she says mean less because she has no degree yet? Can she help me by saying something so aware and wise that I wake up inside myself a little, self-reflect, see something from a new perspective, and then live life differently? You bet.

So, my brave, talented, skilled healer . . . no matter who you are or what life experience you have, you help people in ways you'll never know. The self-doubt does nothing for you or the people who might enjoy your wisdom. Don't keep the world from benefitting from your brilliance because you're feeling not good enough. It's boring.

Let's talk about perfectionism next. It will paralyze you. Don't let it be an excuse.

CHAPTER 14

I'm Not Ready; It's Not Perfect

If there's one fear I'd love for you to have more fun with, it's the perfection paralysis syndrome. *It's not good enough yet, I'm not ready yet,* and *it's not perfect yet* are all versions of the same fear voice in your head that has you never moving forward to make the necessary mistakes that you need to make to get you there. Let the current state of whatever it is be enough, and do it anyway. Watch how the learning, growing, and evolution happen from that brave action you take.

When I wrote and published my first memoir, it certainly was not perfect. I had three friends (one was my mom) proofread the book, and I published with that amount of editing. I spelled Tae Kwon Do wrong. And nobody told me that little bit of info, not even the editors at the self-publishing house I was using at the time.

At least I can chalk that one up to not knowing better. And, of course, I know better now, so I can do better. But if I'd listened to the "this isn't perfect or good enough yet" voice, that really important part of my journey wouldn't have occurred. And the learning, triggering, awakening, and evolution that happened as a result of that imperfect action would have been stalled.

Do it imperfectly. Because perfect is a judgment. And who are you letting define "perfect" for you anyhow? Since publishing my first book, I've learned how to improve each book that's come after. I've learned so many things about improving my writing, my titles, my design, my proofreading, and my editing. With that knowledge, the next book will for sure shine. And I'm so glad the first one moved into the world as imperfect as it was, to be one of my greatest teachers.

That book—and the courage it took to publish words about my life for the world to read—was the beginning of the Brave Healer Revolution. It was important that it come into the world exactly how it did, looking like it did. I would not take any of it back, even for greater perfection.

Taking Action with Perfectionism

The fear of not being fully prepared or ready because the thing isn't perfect is something you'll need to try to get over. It's similar to having a baby; you can tell someone who's never had a baby anything you feel like, but the advice isn't really going to make them any more ready.

Back in 2016, I was asked to do some homework for a coaching mastermind I was enrolled in. We were all working on our businesses, and specifically our online programs. The homework was to write the content, create the platform, and then advertise and launch it as a BETA. A BETA is when you're basically telling the world that this is the first time you've done this and admitting you're not going to be perfect at it.

"I want you all to start a BETA program for your signature course." My coach at the time had twelve of us who were motivated to create and launch an online course for our audiences. "You'll do a twelve-week program, write the content, market it as a BETA program, and get this off the ground," she instructed, giving us the blueprint for what would be the start of something amazing.

I was the only one of the twelve who took action with my first rough content draft and an idea for *The Brave Healers Mastermind*. I wrote out twelve teaching modules, created a sales page and an opt-in page, and then blasted Facebook with the announcement for the BETA program, running at a special discount because it was my first time doing it. In other words, I told people straight up, "This won't be perfect, and you'll get a hand in creating this with me!"

I'll be forever grateful to that coach for giving us that homework. It was through the mistakes, failures, and imperfect content that my current course, *Intuitive Writing and Speaking for Healer Entrepreneurs*, was born, and it continues to evolve and sell out.

I had to take action knowing that my modules were an experiment, that my content was a first draft, that I'd learn how to run the technological pieces I'd never tried before, and that I was probably going to have non-ideal clients in the program. It was the greatest experience ever. Over the course of the twelve weeks, armed with a lot of great feedback from the participants, I went on to tweak, shift, and grow the course into what it is today.

I honestly couldn't believe that out of a dozen women in that program, I was the only one who went through with the homework. And now, several years later, I have at least half a dozen workshops under my belt, each one better than the last.

If I'd waited until the program was perfect or I felt ready to run it, I'd probably still be waiting. The action was the magic of learning. By doing the program and calling it a BETA program, the gals who signed up were fully aware they were being used as guinea pigs of sorts and that I'd be relying heavily on them for feedback for future courses.

Sometimes you just have to do it—imperfectly, but with great intentions—so that you can work on making it better. Making a decision to run that program was one of the best decisions of my life. I now have a community of women who have taken my classes, are having wonderful experiences, and are talking about those experiences to their peers.

I came to the conclusion that it wasn't about being perfect anymore. It was about offering my gifts and learning, growing, and evolving while

I was sharing them. I learned through the doing. I learned through the things that worked, and the things that didn't. I learned by experimenting, trying new things, following my intuition, and taking some risks.

And remember, no decision is a decision. Only it doesn't get you anywhere very fast. When people say to me, "I'm having a hard time making a decision about this because I don't feel ready," I usually encourage them to make any decision. Because some kind of decision will be the way the next best step actually becomes clear.

It's in the action that you put the wheels in motion to get the answer you need. And remember to connect to how it feels. The best way to make a decision is to go back to what you know about what feels good and what feels bad to you. Remember that from Chapter 2? And remember the shortcut to the feeling of confusion, or fogginess . . . that's a no.

We second-guess our own intuition many times. The more you practice, the more you trust, the easier the decisions become. When would I have been more ready to do all that course creation? I don't know. I could have learned more about Zoom beforehand. I could have hired an assistant beforehand. I could have researched about online course platforms more. I could have taken a "creating an online course" course. But I did none of those things. I took my idea and ran with it, learning along the way. I did it even though it wasn't perfect and I wasn't really ready.

It's through the action of creating that you'll learn what you need to learn. It's through the feedback you get, if you're awake enough to listen, that you'll be able to know your next best step. I've learned to sign up for the race before I'm trained. Because there's absolutely no better incentive to make the training happen than to spend the money and sign up for the race.

Many times, through many projects, I recognized my fear of not being ready enough as purpose-driven fear. Actually, I'd never been more ready, in many instances, to do what I wanted to do. But somehow we talk ourselves out of it. We tell ourselves the story about needing one more week, one more certification, one more degree, one more good experience . . . you get the picture.

Trick here is to feel that kind of fear and move gently anyway. When you hear the voice say, *you're not ready, it's not perfect yet!* You can ask yourself, *what if I was ready? What if I'm good enough?*

Now we're ready for Part Four of this book: the action tool kit. I desperately needed tools in my own journey. But what I needed more than the tools themselves was the practice of using them. My practice led to a discipline or lifestyle of using them every day. And that's when things got way more fun regarding my purpose-driven fear. You're going to enjoy many tools in Part Four. I encourage you to add your own and begin creating ways to succeed with your purpose-driven fear that are unique to your needs. Remember, the tool is cool, but the practice using it is awesome.

Your Bravery Toolkit

In this last section, I'll be sharing six powerful tools to rely on during your practice of having fun with fear. Up until now, you've been using the tool of awareness in combination with journaling to build your foundation. Now we'll add some tools that help you shift, transform, and create by up-leveling the mindset and energy with which you tackle your next-level fears. The goal isn't to have no fear; it's to recognize when fear is purpose-driven, feel it, and do your thing anyway. And then make that the way you live fiercely alive every day. Your magic will be directly proportional to the action you take.

Cracked Open

I am soft,
Powerful.
Kind
and effective.
Effortless
and organized.

I am beautiful,
in my imperfections.
Sexy
because of my scars.

I am quiet,
Strong.
Relaxed
and prepared.
Excited
and balanced.

I am confident
inside my insecurities
magnificent
because of my mistakes.

I am
all the sorrow
and
all the joy.

I am darkness
and light.

I am cracked open
and
empowered.

I am everything
and nothing
and the space between.

I am love.

I
am
ready.

CHAPTER 15

Hell Yes Fear Versus Hell No Fear

Go back to the exercise in Chapter 2 where you described the "Hell Yes!" and "Hell No!" feelings. Study your lists, and add any words that have since come to mind. Get really good at this. This is your intuition talking. The art of mastering the listening and knowing is worth the practice and another deeper chapter for you.

Since nobody taught me how to really listen to my intuition as a kid, I had to learn this later as an adult. It was much later (in my 40's) that a coach sat me down and helped me understand the feeling language that's my intuition. That knowledge was so impactful to me that I wrote a poem about it.

How I Know

You should feel sparks
like butterflies.
You're at home
flying high.

Comfortable
happy
the sun is shining

never crappy.

It's your BFF
your bud
you're safe and sound
in this hood.

We could talk all night
all day
and still have some energy left
ready to play.

If you're drained
or mad
confused
or sad

Annoyed
awkward
or infused
with tight

It's a no.
Stop there.
Please trust
the fight.

Don't worry
don't apologize.
Say, "No thank you."
Try that on for size.

Listen well
to what you feel
your soul is speaking
and it's real.

That coach and I had many conversations that year about how I would know. "Please smell the smoke before your house burns down," she'd say, warning me to listen to the feeling, trust it, and take action. We talked about my marriage many, many times before I took action. She knew. I knew but didn't want to know.

I mostly ignored the feeling, that low level "meh" and resentment, because I was so used to it. I thought it was normal to feel that way. Sad, right? And you might ask yourself right now, what are you tolerating? What form of a "No!" are you letting be normal in your body?

I want you to practice feeling. And in this chapter, I'd love to up-level your game a bit from Chapter 2. I'd like for you to have a discipline of listening to the language of your own soul, so badass that no person, situation, or event can fuck with you and what you know is either good for you or is crushing your spirit.

Exercise 13: Say Yes to You

Body awareness exercise: Find a comfortable place to sit or lie down. If you'd like to listen to a recorded version of this exercise, you'll find that here: https://lauradifranco.com/brave-book-resources/.

Close your eyes and start to connect with your breathing. Clear your mind and anchor into the senses. What do you feel? What sensations do you notice?

Relax your body, unclenching and releasing the weight of your body into the chair or bed. With every exhale, soften, release, relax, and let go a little more. Relax your head, neck, throat, and shoulders. Soften the space behind your eyes, through your jaw, and down through your throat and neck.

As thoughts come, release them and reconnect with the sensations of your body and breath. Relax and soften your chest, upper back, and torso, releasing all the way to your fingertips.

With every exhale, allow your body to get heavier and let go. Relax and soften your low back, belly, hips, buttocks, and thighs. Continue to clear your mind and notice the sensations of your body instead. What do you notice?

Relax and release your legs, knees, and feet. Feel your feet on the floor, the surface of your body on the chair, the clothes on your body, the temperature in the room . . . or whatever other sensation comes into your awareness.

Relax and breathe like this for several more minutes. Take a couple final deep breaths, and slowly open your eyes. Move directly into the writing exercise without a break.

Write it: Set a timer for five minutes and fill in the blank without censoring yourself. When I say yes to something that my body is saying no to, it feels_____.

Speak it: Take a moment after your writing to read the words out loud to yourself, and then make any further notes you can about that feeling. You can add some of the descriptive words to your list from Chapter 2.

What you're going for is a deeper understanding of how your body feels when you're in the moments of your regular day. You're after a black-belt-level mastery of those sensations, thoughts, and awareness so you can practice knowing in any given moment whether or not something or someone is messing with your mojo.

Mastering your awareness will mean you get slapped in the face more often because you'll know so much about what's happening that you'll second-guess your increased level of knowing. It might be little things at first, but then bigger, more important things will happen that you'll look back on with palm to forehead and say to yourself, *Omg, I knew that already.*

The goal instead is to keep that palm away from your head and bask in the knowing action you took based on the message coming from your intuition and inner guide.

Here's a small example. My friend and I were buying tickets to a big music festival and had registered to purchase the first tier of tickets available to a special group. We got the email, set the date in our calendars, and set an alarm on our phones. My friend was going to be in a different location on a mobile phone during the buying phase. I was home on my computer, ready with my finger hovering over the buy button.

"Are you ready?" I texted him. "Are you going to be able to get the purchase through, or do you want me to just buy two tickets and you can pay me back later?"

I knew. There was a message in my head that said something like, *just buy two tickets; he's not going to be able to purchase them on the phone.*

Long, painfully chaotic texting story short, my buy screen came up while his sat spinning in a circle and not coming up. I bought one ticket and got my confirmation while his sat spinning. "Hurry and tell me," I shouted by text. "Do you want me to go back in real quick and get you one?"

"Sure," he texted back.

Because we waited, the Tier Two ticket, the only level left by the time I got back online for his, was one hundred dollars more than Tier One. Fuck.

"Well, we're going to the festival!" Was all I could reply back, knowing that ignoring my little intuitional voice had just cost me, literally, a hundred bucks. Thanks, Universe. I got it.

I could tell you so many more stories like this, some little potatoes, some bigger. But the point is the same each time: listen to that voice, especially when you're getting better at feeling and trusting the feelings. There will come a time when if you don't listen, you'll get reminded that saying yes to something your body just told you was a no will begin to hurt. And it won't be over a music festival. It will mean something much more intense, even life-changing.

Let's finish with an exercise to get your vibe a little higher and help you practice knowing your own bliss. I love me a little gratitude list, but a bliss list? Way more fun.

Exercise : Create Your Bliss List

Body awareness exercise: Find a comfortable place to sit or lie down. If you'd like to listen to a recorded version of this exercise, you'll find that here: https://lauradifranco.com/brave-book-resources/.

Close your eyes and start to connect with your breathing. Clear your mind and anchor into the senses. What do you feel? What sensations do you notice?

Relax your body, unclenching and releasing the weight of your body into the chair or bed. With every exhale, soften, release, relax, and let go a little more. Relax your head, neck, throat, and shoulders. Soften the space behind your eyes, through your jaw, and down through your throat and neck.

As thoughts come, release them and reconnect with the sensations of your body and breath. Relax and soften your chest, upper back, and torso, releasing all the way to your fingertips.

With every exhale, allow your body to get heavier and let go. Relax and soften your low back, belly, hips, buttocks, and thighs. Continue to clear your mind and notice the sensations of your body instead. What do you notice?

Relax and release your legs, knees, and feet. Feel your feet on the floor, the surface of your body on the chair, the clothes on your body, the temperature in the room ... or whatever other sensation comes into your awareness.

Relax and breathe like this for several more minutes. Take a couple final deep breaths, and slowly open your eyes. Move directly into the writing exercise without a break.

Write it: Set a timer for fifteen minutes this time and write without censoring yourself. Tell me about a moment in your life you felt was the biggest "Hell Yes!" Take me into it with your senses. What did you feel, see, taste, smell, hear? I gave you more time on this one because I want you to give me every great detail of this scene.

Speak it: After you're done, read your writing out loud to give yourself the practice of feeling those words one more time. Where in your body do you notice bliss hanging out? What parts are talking to you? Where are you literally tingling with delight? How does it feel to inhabit a body that is in a pure blissed-out state? Knowing this will help you follow it in the future. Knowing these feelings will assist you when you're doubting and starting to let the fear back in. Giving yourself permission to unapologetically follow these kinds of feelings toward doing what you love so much that you lose track of time will create a very different path for you. It might even change your life.

Scary, huh? Many of us have spent a lifetime not allowing ourselves to go into the ecstasy. Time to be brave. And time to get used to being there!

For the next tool, we'll talk about using the feeling of fear as a compass so you know exactly when to move forward and go for the things that will bring you the most bliss.

CHAPTER 16

Using Fear as a Compass

What helped me the most in terms of eventually having more fun with my fear was really getting intimately acquainted with what felt good to me. Then I had to up-level that to feelings that were more than just "good." I had to give myself full permission to feel illegal amounts of joy. I say "illegal" because I hadn't really experimented with that unbridled kind of joy before. I was operating from a mindset conditioned to thinking that kind of joy was "too much" and would somehow get me in trouble. This took some retraining.

This feeling is exactly the feeling you're going for. It's how you'll know to use fear as a compass to point you directly where you need to go to make your dreams come true. This is tricky sometimes. If you've never given yourself permission to feel blissed out, or have attached some kind of negative or toxic meaning to feeling like that, you'll dip your toe in and quickly run in the other direction, expecting some horrible thing to happen. Usually, that horrible thing is what someone else will think about you. But as a kid, there could have been other, worse kinds of consequences for being a little too _____ (you fill in that blank).

What has being too much meant to you in the past? Many understand the rule of being seen and not heard. We were taught to behave appropriately. We were taught not to be too loud, too boisterous, too crazy, too whatever. And then as we grew up, we kept following those rules in all the ways we thought we had to in order to get what we wanted or needed. As a kid, that need typically involved pining for the love and attention of our parents, friends, or loved ones. Think about this now. Isn't it exactly the same feeling as an adult?

Following the rules of "appropriate" from childhood will create a mask so complex, even you can't tell you're wearing it. Behaving like you think you should as an adult creates steel prison bars around your heart and soul. Kind of like in the *Star Wars* scene where Princess Lea and Han Solo are stuck in the garbage compactor, those bars will start to close in on themselves. And pretty soon you'll feel like you're suffocating. The escape route is the awareness that you're doing this to yourself.

We've practiced many different ways to feel fear and all the other associated emotions. Let's get really good now at feeling the joy, bliss, ecstasy, and enthusiasm that are the yin to that yang. Let's be just as great at feeling the joy. Let's know her intimately, be able to have a deeper conversation with her. Let's do an experiment with feeling and knowing the kind of joy that burns so brightly inside you that you wake every morning for the rest of your life knowing what you were born for.

Purpose-driven fear is a feeling that shows you when you're bumping up against something that matters. It tells you when you're standing on the edge of the cliff of your comfort zone. It helps you recognize when your soul is about to take a leap toward freedom. It gives you a way to know exactly what you're on the planet to do.

Purpose-driven fear is a map directing you to the big red X that is the purpose of your life. Nice to have a map, right?

Exercise : Fully Express Your Joy

Body Awareness: Okay, by now you're pretty good at this. Realize how quickly you can take a deep breath and arrive in your body like you've been practicing in all of the exercises. You can do this with your eyes open. You can do this at a moment's notice. So do it now. Connect with your body through a few easy, mind-clearing breaths.

Write it: Set a timer for five minutes and answer this question: Where in my life am I still shrinking away from joy? Or, see if this one works better: Is there still a negative or toxic meaning that comes up when I'm living in full, unapologetic expression in the world?

As usual, don't get stuck on the words of the prompt. Just let what's there flow from the inside to the outside without censoring yourself. If you begin to think too much and stop feeling, take another breath, reconnect to your body, and then start writing again. Move the words, messages, and ideas coming through to the page, no matter what they are or if they seem related to the prompt or not.

Speak it: Now take a few moments to read your written words out loud to yourself. Write a little more about how that felt if you want to.

My repeating thought pattern and limiting belief is *this isn't good enough,* or *you're not good enough.* The harsher one is *this will make you look stupid,* or *you're stupid.* What the habitual patterns of negative thought all lead to is *nobody will love you,* or *you'll never be good enough to be loved.*

So when these feelings come up in my gut and chest, I know them well. I named the voice. I stopped making the choking feeling in my throat mean anything more than *you're on the right track; keep moving through this.* I was able to see the pattern of thoughts, particularly my worst self-sabotaging ones, and use them to align with what was in front of me.

The worst time I have nowadays is when I'm about to step onto the stage. In those moments, my body tells me I'm about to die. My face flushes, my heart starts to pound, and then my mind literally goes nuts with messages that try to convince me I'll forget my lines, look like an idiot, and fail. I'm convinced that they'll feel sorry for me.

When you see me on stage sometime, know this is what's happening inside my body. But also know that I've recognized the voices, made friends with the feelings, and mastered the action-taking to the point that I'm not nauseous anymore. I've mastered the game well enough that my legs carry me to the stage and words come out, despite the visceral feelings and inner messages that try to help me survive the perceived attack.

My purpose-driven fear is something I'm so grateful for today. It helps me keep it all real. The awareness helps me communicate with clients, my family, and strangers; it helps me get through difficult situations with people who matter to me, when I feel like giving up, and when I think nothing is working out. The awareness always gives me a choice to respond to life and aim those responses at what feeds my soul.

CHAPTER 17

Flipping the Switch

There's an idea floating around that practicing awareness gives you a choice to switch from any fear-based thought or feeling to another feeling that aligns with and serves your joy. Esther Hicks calls this a pivot, and it's a powerful tool. One that I'd like you to master.

We're now talking about bad vibes, the kind of fear that is paralyzing but not purpose-driven. We're now talking about the self-sabotaging thoughts and feelings that you'll tend to get stuck in out of habit.

Speaking of bad vibes, one of the most difficult times in my life was the year I was separated from my husband of twenty years. I asked for the divorce and then, when we separated, he refused to be the one to move out of the house, even though we had two kids in school and I worked from home.

Thing is, in the state of Maryland, to be considered legally divorced, you aren't allowed to have the same address for a full year. So I moved. I found a one-room apartment two miles from my house and every morning at about 5:30 a.m., I'd get up and go home so I could see my kids off to school and work in my home office. Every night after finishing my work and helping the kids with their homework, dinner, or laundry, I'd pack my bag and head back to the apartment to cry and sleep.

Thankfully, I'd already had several tools in my toolbox to get through that trying time in my life. I knew how to practice meditating and breathwork. I knew exercise helped. I watched comedies on Netflix. I called my best friend when I needed an ear. And sometimes I had wine. Yet with all of those tools, I still cried myself to sleep many nights. The pain in my chest and gut didn't really stop. I texted with my kids at night. One night, I brought my daughter to sleep with me in the apartment, on the futon, because she was that upset about being apart from me.

Flipping the switch from depressed and desperate to happy wasn't always an option. Some days I just had to remember to go neutral, to clear my mind and feel my breathing. Because happy wasn't always an option, despite my tools, my knowledge, and my awareness. But I knew it was always my choice. I could focus on things that helped me relax, or smile, or laugh. And if none of that worked, I could choose to just feel and breathe. And then I started listening to Esther. Esther Hicks and her *PureJOY* videos became my go-to thing to flip my switch to.

When things were feeling difficult, or downright impossible, I'd slide my headphones into the jack and choose one of her lectures to listen to. When Esther Hicks lectures about positive thinking and manifestation, she's always talking about the same thing every time. For some reason, though, there was always a new nugget I took away from listening, no matter how many times I'd heard her talk about love, or money, or relationships, or health.

Esther reminds us that we can't be happy without feeling happy. She helps us understand that there are no conditions for our happiness. That we must feel it first. That we must feel it, period. She talks about the tool of reaching for the best-feeling thought possible, about consciously choosing one and grabbing onto it. And when we do this, she calls it a pivot. I named it flipping the switch.

I like this idea because it's mostly that easy, like walking to the light switch on the wall and consciously pushing that little piece of plastic up or down. When you have an easy tool that's also powerful, it becomes a new practice and habit. When you have a new habit of thought, you are creating a new, powerful belief that you'll base your actions on.

How will you flip the switch when doubt, fear, shame, uncertainty, or any other negative, paralyzing emotion grabs hold of your throat and won't let go? Because I'm a healer, I have to make it clear that I'm not saying to flip the switch as an avoidance tactic. You still feel the feelings fully, allow them to be there, allow them to get bigger if they must, and allow them to rise up to the surface to be released. However, when we're talking about the kinds of fears and old, outdated self-sabotaging messages you're now recognizing as limitations . . . you need a different tool.

When you're aware of a negative thought, emotion, or behavior that does not serve your desire or goal and is not part of the process of healing in a particular moment, you can choose to flip the switch with awareness. Not as a way to avoid feeling, but as a way to feel, understand, and then choose something else. Like joy.

I use a lot of tools for flipping my switch, including those I mentioned at the start of this chapter. And they all do one thing: shift my energy and focus to joy. One of the keys to feeling and being happy is focusing on what lights you up. So what do you do when you've been through something that tosses you into the pit, forces you to feel anxiety instead of joy, and ruins any chances of feeling happy? You recharge, reboot, and refocus. Every day. Until you feel the spark again.

This can happen no matter how much experience you have with awareness and finding your inner joy.

Sometimes we face setbacks and have to get ourselves back on track. Recently, I found myself staring at the blank screen on my computer for weeks, thinking about topics to write about but not being turned on enough by any of them to actually try. That's not because there were a lack of topics, but rather because the emotional rollercoaster I'd been on had kept me deep in my thoughts and kicked me right out of my body, the only place I can choose something else to focus on. I'm a gal who practices this shit for a living, and I found myself lost. How can I teach awareness and healing when I'm so mucked up by the thoughts in my own mind that I've lost myself and my mojo? Well, I decided I'd actually write about it and see if anything useful came up.

We teach what we most need to learn (they say). Anxiety, grief, anger, disappointment, sorrow, doubt, fear, and loneliness all have a way of sucking you into a black hole of unconsciousness. Why? I think it's because this is where we've been taught to dwell. We've been taught that life's hard, it's normal to feel all this negativity, and we should just expect it. We've gotten super great at being sad, angry, depressed, doubtful, and fearful. But what about the joy? I firmly believe we were meant to feel all ends of the spectrum, that life is a playground for our souls, and we get to experiment with all the feels. It's time to get good at joy.

Some days, I feel I've already spent a lifetime practicing feeling anxious. I look around for joy and realize there're a hell of a lot of other people also practicing anxiety (or fear, grief, sadness, or whatever). But . . . joy, people! You know you want it! Energy grows where you put your intention. If I let the paralyzing feelings of anxiety, fear, doubt, shame, grief, and sorrow take over, I'm going to get lost in there.

My personal story is one of divorce, and this might be one of my biggest tests of focus, but I still believe this whole deal can be done differently, with more joy. I'm banking on it. I'm finding that the worse the feelings, the closer I get to the truest place in myself. I'm noticing that the harder it seems to pull myself out of my mind, the more I search for the one place I know I'll get the answers: my own soul. How do you search your own soul? You get quiet. You feel. You listen for answers from your intuition. You surrender. You trust what your body is telling you. And you take action based on those messages.

You choose joy by being aware. One of the students in my writing class was frustrated with this the other night. She understood the awareness piece but still struggled with how to get herself out of the pit once at the bottom of it. She could see and feel the feelings but couldn't understand how to flip the switch to the joy.

"How can I do this?" she asked. "I can't figure out how."

Sometimes I think this is the million-dollar question and wonder when someone else is going to answer it for me. But then I thought about a repetitive part of all the teachings I've read, heard, and learned in the last twenty years and realized the answer is that you have to look within. The answer to how you do that is different for everyone. The techniques and tools you use to pull you out of the pit of grief or fear or whatever other feeling has you stuck, out of your body, and ruminating in those torturous thoughts in your mind are slightly different for each of us. That doesn't mean I'm not going to give you ideas. It means you'll have to read the ideas, see which ones you want to try, take what works, and leave the rest.

And don't give up. Because there're way more ideas than just the ones I'm going to suggest. So when life seems hard, the emotions seem unbearable, and you're desperate to find yourself again—the warrior self that not only feels the intense passion, lightness, gratitude, and fearlessness but lives and breathes it—hear this: You can do this. You're not alone. You need to stay awake. You need to recharge, reboot, and refocus. And you need to practice every day until things shift, without an expectation of a timeline. You need to honor your own process of healing and get super unapologetic about doing what it takes to continue that journey.

Here are ten how's for pulling yourself out of the pit and flipping the switch to the joy:

1. Realize that what's happening is not as bad as what you think about what's happening. In other words, it's in your mind. You're creating a story around your reality, and much of that story can be ditched. Try it. You'll be amazed at what extra baggage you're putting on yourself by putting more meaning into something than is real.

2. Practice using body awareness. Whenever you're feeling the certain way you wish you weren't feeling, first drop all the thoughts in your mind and feel through your body. Let your body do the walking when it comes to the feeling or emotion. Don't think so much. Just feel the physical sensations first, using deep breathing to get you into your body. Try to stay there for several minutes. Do it until there's a shift in feeling or energy.

3. Journal the shit out of what you're feeling. I'm telling you, this will create a door to the answers you seek from your soul. The key to unlocking that door is the writing. Don't censor yourself. Put all the details down on paper. And . . . you can always burn this later, so don't worry about who's going to read it. I'm on book number seven. Seven books' worth of writing! Give yourself a chance to practice this.

4. Move your butt. Literally, move your body. Put some music on and dance. Go for a walk. Go take a yoga class. Wiggle and shake. Lie on the floor and roll around and rock back and forth. Ride a bike. Moving yourself will shift the energy.

5. Go do the thing you love to do. Maybe you paint or write or sing

or dance or do accounting, I don't know . . . but what I do know is that when you're doing the thing that you love, you're very rarely focused on sorrow, fear, doubt, shame, grief, or loneliness.

6. Find someone you can help. When we give to someone else in need, we move out of the story of our own lives and refocus on gratitude by helping someone else. You can help a friend by calling to check on them, or you can help a stranger by volunteering at a homeless shelter. There're a lot of ways to help people.

7. Write a thank-you note. Remember something someone did for you and write them a note of appreciation. The energy of gratitude is powerful and can pull you out of your pit. I sent my best friends and family who supported me through my divorce notes of thanks, and am still thanking them now, much later.

8. Don't believe everything you think. This is another form of awareness that's really important and powerful. I gave my voice a name. So when I hear the thoughts in my head and they're out of control, negative, paralyzing, or otherwise crappy, I talk to her by saying something like, "Hey, Martha, thanks for the input, but you're not being helpful right now. I got this." Lots of what we think is that inner critic voice. Giving her a name will separate you from the voice and give you a powerful tool.

9. Call someone you love and ask for help. Please do this. Not only does talking about your pain help you shift it, the person you called will receive the gift of being able to help you. This is a positive double whammy we don't often realize. Be brave. Reach out. Don't be afraid of asking for help, even if you've asked ten times already; it doesn't matter.

10. And lastly, when nothing seems to help, including the list above, and you feel you've reached a place of grief, desperation, or sorrow you can't pull out of, it might be time to find a professional (therapist or

coach) who can work with you one on one in a powerful, focused manner to create the tools you need to heal. This is difficult work, this healing stuff, and we all need help once in a while. Looking to others for help isn't weakness, it's listening to your intuition about the self-care you need. It's smart as hell. And things will shift very fast when you find someone to guide you.

What are some of the other ways you've flipped your switch? What could you cultivate as your new habit of thought, belief, and action as it relates to your life and who you want to be in it?

Write it: Set a timer for five minutes and make a list of all the ways you can think of to shift your energy or flip the switch when you need to. Then, when you need to, take your list out and pick one! If that one doesn't work, try another!

Next we'll talk about the community you need to build to ensure you're having more fun with your fear and kicking some ass when it comes to living your best life. You don't ever need to do this alone.

CHAPTER 18

Your Badass Community

Build a community of like-minded, heart-centered, awareness-practicing, badass souls and you'll never take another step on this journey without knowing there's someone doing it with you that you can call on whenever you need to.

You'll find a community that I created on Facebook called Brave Badass Healers, a Community for World-Changers.

I don't care where you live or what your situation is, you can begin to grow your community. They can be lifelong friends, family, online friends, colleagues, acquaintances, strangers, or the regular cashier in the grocery store. In fact, you never really know who might be the perfect person to be part of your community until you start putting your real, full-on, authentic self out there, out loud for others to hear.

That's terrifying, isn't it? It doesn't have to be. We're so afraid nobody will "get" or like us. And if you don't really know anyone who gets or likes you yet, you just haven't exposed the real, awesome you to enough people yet. Either that, or you're unconscious and acting from a space of what you think everyone wants to hear.

Your community is the glue that will hold you together when you're falling apart. You must get really good at reaching out when you need them. Your community is the reason you'll wake up and do it all over again. Not having one means a lack of purpose, and purpose is the fuel.

So this is necessary. Unless you're going to go off on your own and do the monk thing. And hey, I get it if you want to do that.

Because monks have it easy, in some ways. No demanding boss. No demanding spouse. No kids in college. No responsibility outside the community they live in.

"The people in the trenches of real, everyday life actually have this much harder than the monks," my healer friend said to me one day. "They are the ones that have the challenges, the triggers, the problems, the constant reminders that doing life with awareness is difficult."

You, my friend, are doing the harder life. Be proud of it. And build a community around you who're doing what you're doing. Find your person, or people. Have lunch. Talk about all the things you want to talk about: life, death, sex, healing, grief, meaning, and purpose. Share your dreams out loud. Stay accountable to your goals with each other. Create collaborations and do some things together. Write a book together. Create an event together. Do joint interviews.

Your community is sometimes how you'll know if you're on track or off. Your community is where you'll find resources and support. They will also buy your books, products, and services. You need a community of badasses to do this.

"The poetry village is real." My friend commented on a fellow poet friend's post on Facebook, and boy, did I feel it. I'd just finished my first feature performance as a poet in August of 2019 I was ecstatic, and the high continued the next day as I read comments on all the posts.

Over the years, my poetry village has grown. I've consciously friended, engaged with, attended the events of, and gotten to know these people. I wanted to build a community of people who love poetry and the healing power of it as much as I do. I needed those particular people to be able to realize my dream of doing that feature. They are why I was there, and they were how I managed to go through with it. They are what helped me get over the purpose-driven fear and deliver my performance in a way that felt amazing.

What community do you need to build? Is it an entrepreneur community? Is it a writing community? A mom community? What support are you looking for? Have you asked anyone yet?

The biggest aha I've come to on this topic is that purpose has a face. When we attach a human face and name to what we do, there's an energy—a big, badass, self-sustaining one. Do yourself a favor and watch my poem video, *Purpose Has a Face*, at http://lauradifranco.com/book-resources/.

It's not *what* you do, it's a *who* you're looking for. Start connecting with people. Who's your Shirley?

CHAPTER 19

Fear-Crushing Affirmations

Affirmations are a powerful way to create the life you crave. I've practiced them forever, but after reading Hal Elrod's book, *The Miracle Morning*, and being inspired by Holly Alexander's *Magic Money Mastery* practices, as well as the powerful practices of Esther Hicks and The Law of Attraction, combined with Jack Canfield's *The Success Principles*—I've discovered some new tips and tricks that are taking this affirmation thing to another badass level. In this chapter, we'll talk about what you're missing in your affirmation game that will change everything.

With awareness, we have a choice to change our internal dialogue. It's the daily—and sometimes hourly—internal dialogue that sets us up for the energy we go about our day emitting. Remember, thoughts are energy. And regular thoughts become beliefs. Thoughts and beliefs spoken out loud become reality when we take action on them.

If you're like me, you've battled your inner critic and fear voices to the point of exhaustion. We've had to do this because of the subconscious, habitual and conditioned way these thoughts and beliefs run our show. And we haven't practiced any alternative tools to counteract them. It's time to reprogram our minds, and affirmations are one way to do it. In fact, they are a powerful way, and after I read some of the amazing authors listed above, I realized a few things I'd been missing:

1. Include a daily affirmation for every area of your life you want to change.

2. Make sure each affirmation is specific and worded positively.

3. Write them down!

4. Read them out loud!

5. Be unwaveringly consistent about this routine!

In the beginning, I followed a few of these steps fairly regularly, but not all of them. I wrote inspiring quotes and affirmations that I came across in my journals and created uplifting social media posts to inspire others, but I wasn't going full-on with these steps. Now I'm excitedly putting into place what I consider to be rocket fuel for my affirmations by creating a consistent, daily ritual that affirms every one of my deepest desires.

To concoct your own affirmation rocket fuel, start following the steps below.

1. Create an affirmation for every area of your life.
First off, don't hold back; start collecting a list of your favorite, most powerful affirmations and/or quotes in a special journal or notebook. I even posted this on Facebook, asking my friends to add to the list to give me some ideas. You might make your own post like that and then copy and paste the list into your phone for easy access. The trick is to include an affirmation that aligns with every area of your life: health, wealth, love, etc. You might even have several affirmations for each area.

When I started looking deeper at my affirmations, I realized I had one for money and one general one that was bravery/worthiness related, but I hadn't taken the time to create special affirmations for things like my love relationship, my community, and my personal and business connections. Affirmations are specific, so it behooves us to create them for each area we want to improve.

2. Word them positively.

This is one of the tricks I learned in my healing and self-development studies that's a game changer for positive thinking and manifesting. Many times, we pray for or affirm things using statements like: *I want to be successful, I want to have a thriving business*, or *I feel pain-free.* The problem with these affirmations is the wording. "I want" means you don't have, so it vibrates with lack. "Pain-free" still has the word "pain" in it.

Instead of saying "I want," word your affirmations positively, for example: *I have everything I need to be successful*, or, *All the resources I need for a thriving business come to me easily*, and/or, *My body, mind, and soul feel healthy, free, and easy.* Challenge yourself to create affirmations that are pure positivity and then up-level your practice by adding that positive emotion, feeling, or vibration when you read them.

3. Write them down!

Many times, we don't take the time to write our affirmations down. It's cool to keep them up in your head, but it's even better when you write them down, because making them "out loud" like that makes them real. Don't skip this! Create a special journal for your affirmations, and even better, take your favorite ones and do something special with them. Post them around your house, place them in picture frames, or decorate them with pretty paper stickers and glitter—whatever it takes for you to notice them more often, read them, and embody their message!

A quick note about experiencing success with affirmations and goals. In Jack Canfield's *The Success Principles* book, he writes about a study done at Yale about goal-setting. In short, the group that had the most success with their goals (76 percent) did three important things: 1) they wrote down their goals, 2) they shared their goals out loud, and 3) they had an accountabilibuddy, meaning they reported in to a friend about their goals every week. We talked about the power of your community in the last chapter. Follow these same steps with your affirmations and watch the magic happen.

4. Read them out loud!

Giving an actual voice to your affirmations is key! Read them out loud. Sing them in the shower. Tell them to a friend. Practice saying them out loud to yourself, and feel the energy and vibration with which you're speaking. The feeling and emotion behind the words is very important. Don't just speak them in a robotic tone or manner. If you're doing that, the affirmation doesn't excite you enough. Pick affirmations that turn you on and make you want to shout them to the world! The ones that make you giggle are the best.

5. Be consistent!

Consistency is the magic juice that will be your rocket fuel. Write them and especially speak them every day, multiple times a day. Get into a routine with this, and stick to it. The more you do this step, the easier it will feel and the more power you'll be putting into what you will be creating.

Consistent, positive affirmations can help you create the life you crave. The practice will begin to change your thinking, beliefs, and behaviors, slowly helping you deprogram the negative ones that don't serve you anymore. This is a powerful step to changing everything and watching your life change before your eyes!

Following are 136 positive affirmations for you to use so you'll always have something when you need it! Affirmations always have a positive energy of joy, love, abundance, and freedom. They are felt and spoken with that energy, as if they are already occurring. You can use these as is, or create your own versions by adding or subtracting a word or two here or there.

Thanks go to Janette Stuart and Holly Alexander for their use, practice, and documentation of the affirmations they've used in their daily lives. There are so many awesome resources, you guys. Find them and, more importantly, use them! Enjoy!

1. I always have enough money to save, spend, share, and give.
2. I have enough money, time, and resources to generously take care of myself and everyone I love.
3. All my decisions are the right ones and move me forward on my path.
4. I trust the journey of my loved ones and feel unattached from it.
5. My thoughts, opinions, beliefs, and ideas feel inspiring.
6. I'm okay.
7. I'm good enough.
8. I'm worthy and worthwhile.
9. All of my investments of time and money come back to me multiplied.
10. My life is exciting and stimulating to me.
11. I'm enough just the way I am and have what it takes to grow into who I want to become.
12. I receive and allow the flow of universal energy through me as I live and serve.
13. I am loved, supported, and protected every step of the way.
14. Things are going great for me.
15. I am love.
16. I am amazing.
17. I am a treasured possession.
18. My timing is perfect and elegant and all is happening in perfect timing.
19. The Universe has my back.
20. Everything is always working out for me.
21. I am the healing space, and I provide rest and restoration.
22. I have everything I need within me.

23. I embrace love, joy, success, and abundance in my life and inspire others to do the same.

24. I am open to giving and receiving love and connection.

25. I'm so happy and grateful that I take care of myself every single day.

26. I can do this.

27. I have everything I need to do everything I want to do.

28. Money comes to me easily.

29. I am powerful beyond measure.

30. I'm a magical, beautiful, powerful goddess.

31. Words come intuitively and easily to me. My relationships are a beautiful product of my awareness.

32. I attract people with amazing hearts.

33. Opportunities abound and show themselves to me every day.

34. I can figure things out when I have to.

35. I'm surrounded by love, support, and joy.

36. I love the feeling of freedom.

37. I love feeling joyful.

38. I attract joy into my life every day.

39. The world feels magical.

40. The people in my life make me feel adored.

41. I'm living my purpose every day.

42. My body feels strong and flexible.

43. I have plenty of energy for everything I want to do.

44. There's nothing I can't figure out.

45. I am so happy and grateful to be alive.

46. I always solve my problems easily.

47. I'm a badass!

48. Answers always come easily.

49. I have incredible gifts to share.

50. My friends and family support everything I do.

51. I feel so grateful for my life.

52. My body moves easily.
53. I'm full of vitality every day.
54. I let go.
55. Everything that happens, happens for me.
56. I'm happily depositing more money into my bank account than I ever dreamed.
57. As money goes out, immediately double the money comes back to me.
58. Money comes to me easily in both expected and unexpected ways.
59. There's more than enough money for me now and forevermore.
60. An abundance of everything I need is always on its way to me.
61. Managing my money is fun and exciting.
62. I am a money magnet. I receive money all the time!
63. I believe I am always divinely guided.
64. My intuition is on point, and I trust it.
65. I know how to make decisions for the best and highest good of all involved.
66. I'm perfect in every imperfection.
67. What else is possible?
68. I'm so excited to see what the day brings.
69. I speak in a way that I'm always clearly understood, and communication is easy.
70. It's easy to express my love to others.
71. I'm so grateful for everything in my life.
72. Things work out in exciting and unexpected ways.
73. The Universe always finds a way to give me what I need.
74. I can't wait to see what happens next.
75. I'm limitless.
76. All is well.
77. Nature invigorates me. I always find nourishment in it.
78. I am supported, protected, and loved, always.

79. I'm so grateful to be able to generously take care of myself and serve from an overflow.
80. I am whole and complete.
81. I easily find the answers to every problem I have.
82. I'm powerful.
83. I'm always learning new things that help me live well and abundantly.
84. Joy is my purpose, and I attract joy easily.
85. I feel empowered in body, mind, and soul.
86. I'm fully capable of creating anything I want for my life.
87. I love nourishing myself with healthy food.
88. I'm smart and allow my intuition to guide my decisions.
89. It's so amazing to celebrate being alive.
90. I'm ready for anything.
91. Everyone I meet is an opportunity to love.
92. I love feeling in love.
93. I love the feeling of gratitude.
94. I love feeling joyful and spontaneous.
95. I'm safe in any decision I make.
96. I'm a powerful communicator and guide.
97. I know what I want, and I love going after it.
98. I'm young, vibrant, and full of energy, no matter how many years I've lived.
99. I love the feeling of living in this body.
100. I love you (said while looking in the mirror).
101. My business connections are thriving.
102. I always meet people who help me on my journey.
103. I feel my purpose burning brightly every day.
104. I thrive doing what I love.
105. My job nourishes me in mind, body, and soul.
106. My co-workers are easy to talk to and always support each other.
107. The resources I need to run my business are always plentiful.

108. I love the way my business is growing.

109. My efforts in time, money, and resources always come back to me tenfold.

110. When I work, it always feels joyful and nourishing.

111. I love having a positive attitude.

112. There's something to feel grateful for every day.

113. I feel so grateful.

114. My family always supports me.

115. New friends appear in my life in unexpected ways.

116. My body feels light, free, and easy.

117. I love the feeling of enthusiasm in me.

118. I love the way it feels to be curious.

119. I'm a powerful creator and healer.

120. I'm worth everything good that comes my way.

121. I feel calm, grounded, and peaceful.

122. I feel easily able to respond to the events of life.

123. I feel sure about my worth in the world.

124. It's easy for me to detach from outcomes.

125. I am. And that's enough. (while looking in the mirror)

126. I can do this!

127. This feels so exciting.

128. This is something I've always wanted to do. I got this.

129. I feel fear but do it anyway.

130. This feeling is telling me exactly what I need to know.

131. I can take action with fear easily.

132. I can always change my mind.

133. What other people think is none of my business.

134. The opinions of others never overpower my intuition.

135. I find my inner wisdom is always guiding me perfectly.

136. I feel encouraged today.

Remember to pick your favorites. Add or subtract words and create your own powerful affirmations that feel specific to your situation. Don't forget that the feeling behind them is the power behind them.

Do you guys remember the book, The Secret? And did you read the sequel to it called The Power? Well, the power behind The Secret is/was love. And, similarly, the power behind your affirmations is the gratitude, love, joy, and abundance energy you feel when you write and recite them. Don't leave that out. If this requires you to fake it until you make it, well, so be it!

In the next chapter, we'll take our affirmations up a notch by adding the powerful tool of visualization to the mix. It's our positive thoughts, out-loud affirmations, and what we practice living in our mind's eye that constitute a powerful shift in how we deal with, overcome, and have way more fun with our purpose-driven fear.

What's after thinking, speaking, and visualizing our turned-on, tapped-in, badass life? Living it **now**. And the book will end on a note to help you do that.

CHAPTER: 20

Visualization

Open up any self-help or success book and you'll find a chapter on visualization. If they forgot that chapter, I'm sorry for them. I'm completely hooked after putting this into practice and experiencing one of the weirdly fastest manifestations of my life.

When I chose to use Liz Gilbert's quote, "Your fear is boring," and really embodied those words, my world changed. My fears shifted to fuel. And my not-good-enough fear seemed funny and totally boring. I took the experiences of my life and the world around me—essentially, what I know about the suffering and the joy—and I realized what I was afraid of didn't make any sense if I wanted to help other people do big things, be seen, share their stories, and gain the exposure they needed to not only build their businesses but leave a legacy with them.

Your fear of not-good-enough is boring, I'd say to myself. And only moments later it was audible, whispered from my lips by something that wanted me to actually hear it so the vibration and power of it would last longer.

I practiced saying it and then visualizing myself being introduced on a loudspeaker. I saw myself walking up onto the stage and addressing a crowd. There was cheering. I could feel the joy-flush in my cheeks. I practiced seeing and feeling this scene every morning upon waking and every evening as I drifted off to sleep.

The next thing I knew, my words were booming out loud from a microphone echoing in every corner of a room filled with nodding women and men. The email to get me there read: "We'd like to invite you to speak to our women's group." And after a quick yes, I began writing and practicing my first big speech that I'd deliver flawlessly to a room of 120 women. I drove home high that day.

Now I want you to decide on the next thing you're going to practice visualizing. What will it be? Is it a scene from your business? Your relationship? Your community? Is it you cashing a check? Having a conversation with an influencer? Closing a big deal? What's the scene you're ready to bring to life? How does it look, feel, taste, smell, and sound?

Remember, your body-mind does not know the difference between something you're actually experiencing and something you're experiencing through visualization. And this is the power of it. If you want to Google the science behind that, have at it. It's out there. Conjuring up a scene in your mind, with all the feels, is creating that reality energetically. Visualization activates your subconscious mind, programs its reticular activating system, and magnetizes you to the people, places, and events you need to achieve your goal.

Convinced there's no way this can work? Then I encourage you to think about all the time you spend worrying. And how many times do your worries come true, at least to some extent? How many times are you short on cash because you're worried about not having enough to pay the bills? How many times do you strike out on love because you're so busy thinking that all the good ones are taken or that you're not lucky enough to find the perfect match?

"I think about worst-case scenarios because I don't want to be disappointed if things don't work out for me," a friend confided to me. And I'm wondering how many people were taught this as a survival tactic. I'm even more excitedly wondering what would happen if we all trained ourselves to think in best-case scenario. More importantly, while we're waiting for whatever we're waiting to happen, doesn't it seem like way more fun to practice best-case scenarios? Why not do that experiment? What's it going to hurt?

This all makes perfect sense to me. It's why I've always been unapologetically positive. And it's why I never conceded when my ex, friends, bosses, or family tried to label that behavior or mindset as irresponsible, unprofessional, or reckless. They can have their opinion. I can have mine. And my body, mind, and soul is way better served by thinking positively—with gratitude, love, and abundance—than by worrying about worst-case scenarios or dwelling on something that is out of my control. People believe what they are used to, conditioned to, and taught to believe. I'm way more interested in noticing what other possibilities there are and staying aware of how I feel when I'm thinking, believing, or acting, especially when I'm trying to create something new for my life.

"When you perform any task in real life, researchers have found, your brain uses the same identical processes it would use if you were only vividly visualizing that activity. In other words, your brain sees no difference whatsoever between visualizing something and actually doing it."
—JACK CANFIELD FROM THE SUCCESS PRINCIPLES

Visualization 101

1. Visualization is easy. Here are the steps:
2. Close your eyes while in a comfortable room without distractions.
3. See yourself in the exact situation you desire.
4. Feel with all of your senses exactly how that situation is going down: sight, smell, sound, taste, and touch.

Add emotions, exactly how you would feel as if this was happening now.

Practice this often.

I don't want to make this any more complicated than I have to, because all I really want you to do is practice. You can do a visualization for any goal you've made for yourself. You can do it for five minutes or twenty. But you really only need a few minutes every day.

Now ask yourself: How badly do I want this thing that I want? Because you're going to need the feeling of inspiration to carry through with the practice of this. The more often you practice, the more powerful the practice becomes, so it's important to prioritize the practice and take time every day for it. And then enjoy the reality of regular good vibes, affirmations, and visualization becoming your regular lifestyle.

I choose to practice for a few minutes every morning, just as I wake, and for a few minutes every night as I'm going to sleep. You can practice anytime, anywhere. No rules. Figure out what works for you.

Now is a great time to revisit your why from Chapter 3. It's the why that creates the drive that fuels a new discipline of badassery for your transformation. How badly do you want this? Enough to sacrifice the things you're used to?

Play With Your Fear and
Heal the World

Sometimes it's our own self-imposed limits that hold us back from being and achieving all we're meant to, as Gay Hendricks talks about in *The Big Leap* (if you haven't read that yet, put it on your list). I was talking to myself about my upper limit problem—that tendency to knock myself back down after an accomplishment—and realized it didn't have to go down like that. I realized that just like every other fucking thing in my life, the upper limit was just an awareness game. And if I have control over anything in this life, it's my own awareness.

When will I crash? I wondered to myself as I hit the play button on the *PureJOY* YouTube channel for my ride home after one of my big talks. *And how will I keep up this level of inspiration?* I wondered. *How will I not fall into the old, conditioned, habitual patterns of thought, belief, and fear that've driven my bus for so long?*

The answer to those questions in my head was in the moment, as I took a breath and hit "send" or clicked "publish" or pressed the big green call button on my iPhone. The answer to my fear was in the action of walking across a stage despite the feeling of slight nausea in my stomach. The answer was in my moment-to-moment decision to say or do, instead of just sit and think and dwell and suffer and fear.

The answer is in who I'm being in this very moment as I'm writing these words. I'm aware, and so I get to choose what to do when my purpose-driven fear shows up as those old boring feelings inside of me. *Wow, I get to choose,* I think. And, *whoa, I get to choose,* I think.

Taking responsibility for everything and moving through the fear to the other side of that wall of fire is both awesome and scary. It will always be both. It's just a matter of who I'm being in the moment of feeling it all. The future me I will thank myself for being is creating herself right *now!* I can't waste time thinking about all the ways I want to be; I must act in those ways now.

We can spend a lifetime thinking about how we'd like things to be, operating from a mindset of lack. Or we can spend our new life thinking about how we'd like things to be, in a mindset of gratitude for the fact it's already ours.

On Flying High

"You killed it! You absolutely killed it." Jeff, my newly-hired performance coach exclaimed as he stood up to give me a hug after the poetry feature at Busboys. As I craned my neck to look up at his over-six-foot-tall body, the smile on his face said everything. I wouldn't let the doubt thoughts in right then. I was too high. I expected them in the car on the way home. They didn't come. I called my mom, as I often do on big nights, to tell her the tale. I felt three years old again, like I'd climbed barefoot up the sides of the door jam and called out, "Look at me, Mom!"

"Hey, honey," she answered. "Hey, Mom! I'm driving home from my poetry feature. Oh my God, it was awesome!"

"Oh honey, that's so great! Were your friends there?" she asked.

"Yes, and I even had a few surprise visitors!" I continued. "There were also some big-time poetry powerhouses that came out to support!" I gushed. I let myself have that moment. Because what I expected was that by the time I was home alone in my fuzzy pants faced with my current housemate's lack of interest in my big night, I'd crash mentally.

I didn't. I slept well. I slept with a smile on my face, even though nobody at home asked me about my big night, and I had to just come out and say to them, "Oh my God, tonight was awesome!" But I didn't crash into any pits of *they don't care* thoughts. The vibe was still so big inside me and the friends who had attended still so powerfully in my heart that nothing, not even my own bullshit self-sabotage, was going to touch it.

The next day, when I slowly opened my eyes in the morning and felt for the familiar feeling of letdown, it was absent. Same with the day after that and the day after *that*. And I didn't spend too much time looking. I knew to move back into feeling the softness of the cotton sheets and the warm skin of my partner next to me instead. Mmm, being here in the now is so, so nice.

Part of the secret to having more fun with fear is to understand that it's always your choice to be in your now. And through awareness, it will continue to always be your choice how you think, what you believe, what you say to yourself, what you say out loud, the energy and attitude you bring into those moments, and then how you go about being all that right now. Right now is the answer to almost everything.

I created a game out of it. When I realized it wasn't just about me anymore, it became about how my courage to tell my story was the spark someone else needed. It became about the possibility of changing or saving or shifting someone else's life. Giving them an aha, catapulting them into purpose, helping them realize—possibly for the first time in their lives—that they are worthy because they were born.

"This is not about you!" The voice, strong in my bones, stands firm. She wants me to relax. She's tired of moving her message through my old, nervous, shaking hands and lips. She has important work to do. I've decided it's okay to get out of her way and let her do it. When you become the vehicle for something bigger, nothing much can touch you anymore: not doubt, not shame, not fear, and certainly not that idea that you're not good enough. Borrrrinnnnng!

Up-leveling your mindset like this changes everything. For you. And for anyone you come in contact with. Feels like a huge responsibility sometimes. But I say, *bring it on!*

When you move forward into the world having fun with your purpose-driven fear, shining the light of your gifts, knowing you're following your purpose, and feeling that inside of you as the biggest, juiciest, most soul-nourishing joy, well . . . that's something I'd like to feel for the rest of my life. I know you would too. And guess what? It's yours for the taking.

What are you choosing, as you close the pages of this book? Try journaling.

What are you choosing as you take your next breath? Try a sigh of relief and joy.

What are you breathing in? Try gratitude.

What does the you who's having way more fun with her boring fears look like? Try on a big smile.

How is she acting right now? Try calling or emailing a friend to share a goal.

What is she saying right now? Try a powerful affirmation.

What is she listening to? Try an Audible book about something positive.

What is she feeling deep inside right now? Try deep-seeded worthiness.

Notice everything. Write it down. Read it out loud. Talk about it to your friends. Initiate conversations that matter to you. Build a community for yourself that helps you wake up every day in the purpose and inspiration of your own life and dreams.

Fear is just a feeling.

Take a deep breath.

Connect with your inner warrior.

Be afraid. And go get your badass on anyway.

I'm here if you need support. The Brave Healer Revolution is about that authentic, inclusive, heart-centered, and sometimes a bit wild and crazy community you've craved . . . maybe your whole life. I needed one. So I created it. And now I'm inviting you to be a part of it.

What's your next step on the journey? Place that foot with awareness, curiosity, gratitude, and love. And a little badass energy. And just keep stepping.

Your fear of not-good-enough is boring. This isn't about you anymore. What if the thing you're still a little afraid to say or do is exactly what someone else needs to hear or see to change or even save their life? It's time to be brave.

CHAPTER: 22

Your Wild and Precious Life

*"Tell me, what will you do with
your one wild and precious life?"*
—MARY OLIVER

"And so it is! This or something better!" My first life/business/spiritual coach would always say this line whenever we stated a desire. And it reminds me to remind you to be everything you desire. Be it now. Live these things in the ways you can every day. Stop wishing and be it. Stop wanting and say it. Stop wondering and find it out. Stop hoping and take some small action.

Inside of those small ways of being, you will be able to recognize that you're actually everything you want to be, right now. When that happens, you'll feel like someone's tapping you on the head with a magic wand and saying, "Wish granted." The gratitude should flood into your cells and fill you to overflowing.

Double-check your mindset every single time the thoughts move south toward negativity. You'll get caught up in the tough ones. "You're not being realistic," is one that's tough for me. When that gets thrown around, I laugh a little. Your reality is not my reality. Just because you think that something is unrealistic doesn't mean I have to believe it.

Claim your wants and desires, but remember to reverse-journal them right away and then use them as affirmations. Here's an example.

Want: I want a thriving business that helps me pay the bills and take care of those I love.

Reverse-journaled affirmation: I'm so happy and grateful to be running a thriving business that easily covers the bills and allows me to generously take care of myself and everyone I love, and then some!

"And so it is," means you're speaking and living it into existence. You're living into the life you desire in thought, word, and action whenever you can. And when you're not totally there, you're acting as if you are.

Remember, your daily routine offers multiple opportunities to live into your dream. Those opportunities include the way you dress; whom you hang around with; the calls and emails you make; the food you eat; the way you keep your house, car and belongings; whom you have lunch with; the conversations you take part in; what you tell others you'll do; what you actually do; the invitations you accept; the places you go; and every person with whom you interact. Every day offers an opportunity to be the person you were meant to be.

If fear usually paralyzes you, respond in a new way. If you don't normally speak up in a conversation with your spouse, try voicing your thoughts. If you don't normally wake up early to exercise, set a new schedule. Not in a habit of eating healthy food? Eat healthier today. Break the old patterns and start living in a new way, today.

Thoughts of "I want this kind of life" usually means you're not making the decision to live that life to the best of your ability with the resources you have right now. When it comes to your purpose-driven fear and being the person you know you were born to be, many times it's about choosing a different way to respond when you feel the old feeling.

That might include switching your thoughts to, *What an amazing life I'm living! And so it is!* And actually, think about it for a moment: you are living an amazing life, aren't you? There is so much to be grateful for. If you're alive, things are good. If you have a roof over your head and more than one pair of shoes, consider yourself damn lucky. Everything is relative, and there's always a perspective that helps you feel into that amazing feeling of goodness and gratitude.

One final note to help you understand how to make all of this come together and see the results you are hoping for: nothing works unless you do. Get to it. Take some action. You don't have to be ready, perfect, confident, motivated, or fearless. You just need to move your ass, even if you have to do it without those feelings backing you up. As soon as you figure out how to take the action even when you don't feel like it, you'll be on the road to success, in every way possible. As soon as you clear your mind of the worry about what anyone else will think and you take the action that makes your heart sing, whether or not you might fail, you'll be on the journey to joy that most people never take.

Most people wait for the confidence, courage, or motivation to take action. And that's the problem. You don't get those feelings without taking the action. The action is the way you cultivate those things. Having fun with your fear is what you must do so that you live the experiences that will help you realize every big dream.

Life gets very interesting when you play in your discomfort zone and invite fear into the sandbox with you. I see you there, brave healer. I hear your message. It matters. Keep sharing it. You are changing the world, one brave thought, belief, word, and action at a time. I'm so honored to be on this journey with you.

Resources

I've listed many of my favorite resources here for you. Create a strategy in which what you consume on a daily basis, in terms of books, television, audio, conversations, etc., is feeding your soul. Don't settle for anything that doesn't fill you with joy, or worse, brings you down. Life's too short for that shit. Having fun with fear is about awareness. These resources will help with that.

BOOKS:

Bessel van der Kolk, M.D.—*The Body Keeps the Score*

Bruce Lipton, Ph.D.—*The Wisdom of Your Cells*

Bruce Lipton, Ph.D.—*The Biology of Belief*

Dr. Joe Dispenza—*Breaking the Habit of Being Yourself*

Peter Levine—*Waking the Tiger*

Brené Brown, Ph.D., LMSW—*Daring Greatly*

Lissa Rankin, M.D.—*The Fear Cure*

John F. Barnes, PT—*Healing Ancient Wounds*

Adyashanti—*True Meditation*

Gay Hendricks—*The Big Leap*

Rhonda Byrne—*The Secret*

Rhonda Byrne—*The Power*

Anthony de Mello—*Awareness*

Eckhart Tolle—*A New Earth*

Suzanne Scurlock-Durana—*Full Body Presence*

Ingrid Bacci, Ph.D.—*The Art of Effortless Living*

Ted Larkins—*Get to be Happy*

Jack Canfield—*The Success Principles*

Marie Forleo—*Everything is Figureoutable*

Denise Duffield-Thomas—*Chillpreneur*

MEDITATIONS/AUDIOS:

The *Calm* app

www.ListeningtoSmile.com has some great sound healing music. (Use the code BRAVE 19 for 40% off!)

VIDEOS:

Find the Brave Healer Productions channel on YouTube

Find Abraham Hicks videos at www.AbrahamHicks.com
KyleCease.com (love his inspirational and spiritual stuff!)

COMMUNITIES:

Brave Badass Healers, a Community for World Changers Facebook group

The On Purpose Woman Community:
www.onpurposewomancommunity.com

The Wellness Universe online community:
www.TheWellnessUniverse.com

Success Champions (Where Badass Business Owners Network)
Facebook group

Postscript

But wait, there's more. I get that fear is tricky. I get that making statements like, "Your fear is boring" is bold and might sound compassionless. But can you recognize moments in your life when you had to be shook awake? When the Universe had to slap you in the face a little to get you to understand what you needed to do? I've known a few of those moments.

When my daughter came to me this year—the year I was to publish this book about fear—to let me know she'd been hurt by someone we called a family friend, I questioned everything I knew and was teaching about fear. I lost myself, my mission, my purpose, and my mind for a couple months while we navigated a disgusting and awful road I'd never dreamed I'd be walking with her.

And then the coronavirus hit. My already totally-shredded, spent, exhausted mind, heart, and soul had to start to deal with the stress that ensued as a result of my hands-on physical therapy business being shut down, schools being closed, and the rest of those dominoes. "Really, Universe?" I questioned, "Wasn't the first thing enough?"

There are pieces of the journey we will walk for months more during these crises. In the end, it's the awareness that will serve us, heal us, and shift us toward joy. It's the awareness and the choice we get when we make it our lifestyle, to turn our faces toward the sun, stand up tall inside our worthiness, share our truth, take fear by the hand, and say, "Don't worry, we got this."

And, as I type these last words to you here, I continue to walk my walk of leading those who know that sharing their story is how they'll heal, and how they'll change the world. What happens to us, happens for us. I know this. And even if I can't see that right in the moment of my pain and worry, I know the bigger picture is being orchestrated by something much more powerful than me. I also know I'm a part, a spark of that powerful energy. Fear is a feeling I know is here to serve me, and my power lies in my ability to tell my story out loud, even if I have to shake while I do it, again.

Brave Healer. Yes, yes I am. And so are you.

A Rampage of Gratitude

I'm incredibly grateful to so many people for helping me with this book. Thank you Christy Collins for your magical cover and interior design. Thank you Steve Harrison for helping inspire the business behind this book, and for introducing me to Jack Canfield. Thank you Martha Bullen for your stellar book coaching. Thank you Honorée Corder for your help with all things book business, and badass book strategy, and for your unexpected texts that always help me know I'm not alone. Thank you to the Brave Healer Book Launch Warriors book launch team who gathered to support me and this message.

Thank you Jonathan and Danielle for supporting me during this crazy year of transition and chaos. You two are the brightest lights in my life and inspire me to be the best I can be every single day. Thank you Chris for standing by my side while I worked my way through the doubt. Thank you Shelly for helping me believe in myself every step of the way and for always being ready to celebrate the wins. Mom, I love you. Your support throughout my life has meant everything to me.

Master Holloway, your encouragement to "discipline the mind" has been so powerful for me on this journey. I'm grateful to have studied with you and our Gentle East family.

And to you Brave Healers: thank you for trusting me to guide you through the fear. The brave words I write are inspired by you, and my deep desire to see you thrive.

About the Author

LAURA DI FRANCO, MPT, is the owner of Brave Healer Productions, where she leads a powerful community of badasses learning to spread their message of health and empowerment in much bigger ways. Laura has three decades of expertise in holistic physical therapy and, with a third-degree black belt and eighteen published books, she has a clear preference for traveling fast and being badass, but she's also the champion of small business owners who want to push their health-based practices to the next level. Through her Maryland-based business, Laura inspires through speeches, workshops, a writing club, and other services that help talented health professionals tell their own stories so they too can maximize their professional impact.

Laura lives her mission every day, but when it's time for some R&R, you'll find her driving her convertible Mustang, taste-testing dark chocolate, or bouncing up and down at a rave with her beau. Pop over to BraveHealer.com and share your story of having more fun with your fear. Who knows, you might just find yourself in her next blog or book!

Other books by Laura Di Franco

Living, Healing and Tae Kwon Do: A Memoir to Inspire Your Inner Warrior

Brave Healing: A Guide for Your Journey

Your High Vibe Business: A Strategic Workbook for Badass Entrepreneurial Success

The Ultimate Guide to Self-Healing Techniques: 25 Home Practices & Tools for Peak Holistic Health and Wellness

The Ultimate Guide to Self-Healing Volume 2

The Ultimate Guide to Self-Healing Volume 3

The Ultimate Guide to Self-Healing Volume 4

Joy Stacking: The 3-Step Formula for Authentic Success

Warrior Love: A Journal to Inspire Your Fiercely Alive Whole Self

Warrior Joy: A Journal to Inspire Your Fiercely Alive Whole Self

Warrior Soul: A Journal to Inspire Your Fiercely Alive Whole Self

Warrior Dreams: A Journal to Inspire Your Fiercely Alive Whole Self

Warrior Desire: Love Poems to Inspire Your Fiercely Alive Whole Self

Other books published
by Brave Healer Productions

The Wellness Universe Guide to Complete Self-Care: 25 Tools for Stress Relief, by Anna Pereira

The Wellness Universe Guide to Complete Self-Care: 25 Tools for Happiness by Anna Pereira

Find Your Voice, Save Your Life by Dianna Leeder

Join the AUTHOR TEAM for the next Ultimate Guide to Self-Healing book!

Brave Healer Productions is now accepting applications to be part of our next book!

You're a healer . . .

. . . and a business owner, and you're ready to share your message with the world in a bigger way!

Contributing a chapter to this powerful collaborative project is much more than just having your name on a book.

It's about being part of a community of healthcare entrepreneurs who are changing the world with their brave words and tools.

Each author shares their story, and teaches an effective self-healing tool in their chapter. Authors then have opportunities to do live training, podcast interviews, and business development activities as a part of the Brave Healer Productions family.

We can't wait to hear your story!

Submit your application today!
https://lauradifranco.com/ultimate-guide-project/

"All I can say is, if you have a book inside you, a message you want to gift the world, or a healing business you want to grow, there is no one better than Laura Di Franco, and Brave Healer Productions. She and her team will guide you through all the stages, from concept to writing to getting your book into the hands of your readers. She genuinely wants to bring health and healing to the world we all live in. And she delivers big time."

—DR. SHELLEY ASTROF, AUTHOR OF *THE KNOWER CURRICULUM*

"It's one thing to have a process that will help a book become successful. It's a whole other thing to create success from a place of holding sacred space and unconditional warrior love for every person she works with to step into their capacity for brilliance. My heart is grateful for the innumerable ways Laura has created for authors to connect with readers."

—SHARON CARNE, DIRECTOR OF TRAINING AND DEVELOPMENT, SOUND WELLNESS

"Laura Di Franco is a master at helping your work take flight and land with your target audience. She has a unique ability to help you draw out your good ideas, and her experience in the world of writing quickly moves ideas to action. Laura has no shortage of ideas for your success and will give you more than you could imagine possible. Trust her to land your words!"

—DR. ERIKA PUTNAM, DC, RYT 500

Submit your story idea here:
https://lauradifranco.com/ultimate-guide-project/

Your words will change the world when you're
brave enough to share them.
Your fear of not-good-enough is boring.
What if the thing you're still a little afraid to share
is exactly what someone needs to hear to change,
or even save their life?
It's time to be brave.

—LAURA DI FRANCO

www.ingramcontent.com/pod-product-compliance
Lightning Source LLC
Chambersburg PA
CBHW061152120626
46546CB00005B/2032